There Are Only 7 Ways to Meditate

Make Your Meditation Amazing

Q.C. Ellis

All One Planet

Copyright © 2022 by Q.C. Ellis and All One Planet Ltd

All rights reserved.

No portion of this book may be reproduced in any form without written permission from the publisher or author, except as permitted by U.K. copyright law.

Contents

Foreword	V
PART ONE - Be an IntrAnaut	1
1. First Steps into the Journey	2
2. What Is an IntrAnaut?	7
3. What Is Meditation?	11
4. Formal v Informal Practice (and Myths)	18
PART TWO - 7 Ways to Meditate	24
5. Restful Absorption (RA)	25
6. Myth: I Cannot Meditate	36
7. Intentional Awareness (IA)	40
8. Myth: Try Hard to Succeed	48
9. Engrossed Attention (EA)	56
10. Myth: Meditation Is Too Difficult	70
11. Attitude	75
12. Authentic Attitudes (AA)	85
13. Myth: I Cannot Visualise	102
14. Visualisation or Imagination (VI)	106
15. Myth: I Don't Have Enough Time to Meditate	112

16. Question or Introspect (QI)	116
17. Myth: You Can Never Fall Back	123
18. Mantra or Invocation (MI)	128
PART THREE - Next Steps	136
19. Frequently Asked Questions	137
20. Get into the Habit	145
21. Resources and What Next?	151
Glossary	164
About the Author	171
Acknowledgments	174

Foreword

by Norma Foster

For as long as I can remember, I've been curious to understand the why and the how. I wanted to discover hidden layers in each experience, and to learn how to deepen my relationship with others and the larger world.

A severe head concussion in 2011 turned that curiosity into a search for healing, inner peace, and resilience. It led me to meditation and the work of Dr Joe Dispenza. His piece in the movie, *What The Bleep* had impressed me greatly, talking about how to create your day and your reality.

I read *Evolve Your Brain* and was captivated. The science, combined with thousands of stories of spontaneous healings, was compelling. I sat in my designated healing chair every day and, with my sore brain, gave this thing called meditation its best shot. And I took it seriously – I read so many books – and devoured all the research and data I could get my hands on.

I did all the courses and workshops that I could afford around the globe. My first event with Dr Joe Dispenza was in Basel, and it was weeks before my feet came back down to ground level. There were many more in between.

Dr Joe is dedicated to bringing science to the art of meditation because knowledge and understanding empower us. He has done scientific tests on over 8 thousand meditators at his events over the years.

I've had many brain scans, 24-hour heart monitors applied, and GDV testing done before and after the week-long retreats. I have seen the evidence of the benefits and wonders from meditating, and it is compelling.

At some level, and rather naively in the early days, I expected my spiritual journey and progress with meditation to be fairly consistent. And then I experienced another healing crisis in 2018.

My anxiety and insomnia had reached such levels that I could no longer meditate, let alone sleep properly. For many long months, I was devastated and couldn't see a way out.

It was at this point that I first met Colin (author Q.C. Ellis), at a 5 Rhythms Dance class in Newcastle (in the UK). I had heard of his gifts and experience as a meditation teacher and coach and asked for his help and advice. I trusted him immediately. We talked at length. He taught me (and used) tools and techniques I could relate to. They helped enormously.

I realised I had understood so much over the last seven years. Mostly from a logical perspective of the learning and training. However, that was when I had been in a good place.

I also realised I had pushed myself through most of the difficult experiences in my life. The ability to meditate and do the inner work when not in a good place brought me a deeper level of understanding. Borne of experience, not the logic.

I learned how to accept my fears at a deep level, observe them, and let them go. This is a daily practice, and the work is never done. It's a journey, never about the destination, and that journey starts with yourself.

Meditation helped me to liberate my own inherent power and helped me to appreciate my capability to release it in other people. Meditation created a massive paradigm shift. It has been transformational in both my personal and professional life.

I went on to do many meditations with Colin. Retreats in Scotland and Cumbria, which were truly wonderful. I'll never forget that epic walk, where his words helped me to transform the worst of days. That day, I began to learn the beauty of the present moment. That my experience of life can change dramatically in each moment.

Colin eloquently set out his vision of what life is in a way that I could truly appreciate. The saying, "What if your worst day is your best day" took on a whole new meaning for me! Every generous present moment is a new beginning. And so it was!

Then I became a student of his meditation teacher training course. His breadth of skills, knowledge, and training are extensive. He is a very genuine, sincere, and trustworthy person. I am deeply grateful for his support and care, and his thoughtful, wise words of guidance.

We have supported each other in our work together. I'm now ready to be a part of the support team again at the next Dr Joe Dispenza workshop, where we expect 2.4k meditators.

Colin can help you master your practice, reduce stress, boost health and wellbeing, and ultimately transform your life. He has drawn the best from every style and school he has studied.

Tony Robbins was once asked, "What's the secret to achieving results? The secret to lasting change?" And his answer is always the same, "You must train yourself to become a master... that takes consistency, commitment, and focus."

That's what this book offers. Dynamic tools, techniques, and practices. A guide to help you create lasting change in your meditation practice. Ultimately, to transform the quality of your life.

You will find many things in this wonderful book that will help you. And what more can anyone ask from a book?

Between this and the follow-on book, I think there is the wisdom of great spiritual truths. Colin sets them out in a sincere and practical way. He is devoted to pursuing and sharing his highest knowledge and truth.

I know my experience with meditation is so much richer for having learned from Colin.

~ Norma Foster, *International Growth Consultant and Therapeutic Coach*

For more resources, download the mobile app, provided by the author and IntrAnaut™ Academy.

With your **Android** Smartphone, point your camera at the QR code below and choose your QR code reader (e.g., Google Lens), to be taken to Google Play

With your **Apple** Smartphone, point your camera at the QR code below and choose your QR code reader, to be taken to Apple Store

There is a CODE at the end of the chapter, *Resources And What Next?*, so you can access exclusive content on the app, including the audio meditations from the book. If you cannot access the app, subscribe to the **All One Planet newsletter** to access the material and courses via websites. www.**qcellis.com/7-ways-newsletter**

PART ONE - Be an IntrAnaut

Use meditation to de-stress and heal - attain a happier, fulfilled life - or awaken your personal evolution

1
First Steps into the Journey

THIS BOOK IS FOR a special group of people. People like me, who tried meditation but found it difficult to gain the benefits. In fact, it may have even felt detrimental to continue with the practice. Also, those who are still meditating, maybe sporadically, but not gaining the benefits they see others achieve.

After decades of frustration, my dogged persistence has paid off. By making every error, I know the sneaky ways we can trip ourselves up. By knowing how to change your practice in subtle ways, it can work for you.

Within these pages is a framework upon which to develop your practice. The framework has two parts:

- Seven *spheres* of meditation. They are the *forms, ways, types, or mind-technologies* of meditation. You'll find them within this book.

- Seven secret codes, or principles (to be found in the follow-on book, *7 Secret Codes of Meditation*).

The seven spheres are the only ways to meditate, because they are the seven *mind-technologies of meditation*. You cannot meditate without using at least two of these mind-technologies. Therefore, the seven spheres encompass all meditations (every one of the 1000s of meditations utilise at least the core two mind-technologies). They are the practices to attain the fruits of meditation.

The seven secret codes are the principles that underpin your practice.

With these two layers of understanding, you see what is happening within your meditation, and your next step is obvious. If there is a problem, this framework helps you diagnose the issue and offers straightforward solutions.

This guide assists meditators in overcoming obstacles such as: "I don't have enough time to meditate", or "My mind is too busy to meditate", or "I cannot visualise"; and the list goes on.

Exploring each of the seven spheres/forms/mind-technologies of meditation will assist you in recognising which meditation styles will help you in your goals and life. With this guide, you will know when you are doing it right and can feel confident you are meditating properly. It is a vast subject, but I aim to not only answer the most common questions but also give you a clear understanding that is practical and makes sense.

A New Framework

I'm sharing with you the framework I created so my Meditation Teacher College students can lead sessions with confidence. Now, I see aspiring teachers, who only had fragments of the picture, shine with authenticity, self-assurance, and mastery. They derived a substantial part of that authority from the framework you have in your hands.

Within this compact book, you will discover:

- The inside scoop on all seven mind-technologies that are the spheres of practice we call meditation.

- An easy meditation for each of the seven spheres.

- The mistaken beliefs about meditation that could stop you from gaining all the benefits.

Meditation is simple, yet there are tripwires that can stop you. Navigate around them using my guidance and progress in your meditation practice. It is time to leave the obstacles behind and start meditating. You can use the seven mind-technologies of meditation to enrich your life, and be happier, content, and fulfilled.

You can find extra resources on the free mobile app, Meditation & Wellbeing. Find out more and download the app at www.MeditationWellbeing.app

There is also a code at the back of the book (in chapter 21, Resources & What Next), so you may access exclusive content on the app, plus the meditations within this book on audio.

How Did You Get Here, Colin?

A book fell out off the shelf at the library. It listed many personal development courses and organisations. Several intrigued me. Not least, the potential to facilitate healing through your hands. This was before Reiki became popular.

I'm not into blind faith, so was pleased to find a course on Therapeutic Touch that was non-denominational. A year into my two-year probationary period, I was told by my mentors that I should meditate. I wondered who might be the best people to teach me. In 1998, I began my journey into meditation.

After my initial fumbling, almost every sentence from the monks and nuns seemed to reveal hidden perspectives. These nuggets of understanding gave way to finding gems of knowledge as I dug deep into the practice.

In 2001, I felt I'd reached a level of mastery. Mostly because of two (nine and six months) silent and solitary Buddhist retreats with the guidance of a venerable Tibetan monk.

Six months later, my life fell apart. While in a stressful job, panic attacks engulfed me and my doctor diagnosed stress and anxiety. My mind became very pedantic, pessimistic, and sceptical of everything – including meditation.

It threw me into a snake-infested pit of despair. I found it almost impossible to do formal meditation. The peaks previously visited vaporised into dreams of a former life.

I began exploring meditation again from the ground up. By the time I decided I knew enough to teach meditation, another decade had gone by. Several three-to-twelve-month retreats in solitary and silence were a part of that journey to feeling capable of teaching meditation. I explored other Buddhist traditions and other spiritual paths. It must have been about 2008 when I created the popular course, *Meditation: ABC*.

A decade later, I was being encouraged to set up a course for aspiring meditation teachers. Yes, I had a style of teaching that seemed at odds with many who teach meditation. I had created new ways of exploring meditation to give students a thorough understanding right from the start.

It helped that I'd previously developed certified courses as a college lecturer. They were on personal growth and verified by national accreditation bodies. I had also become an Assessor of others' self-improvement programmes. Yet, when thinking of training people to become meditation teachers, I still felt like a fraud.

A charity asked me to facilitate their anxiety group, but a mindfulness teacher told them, "Colin is not qualified!" Thankfully, I was getting significant results with the group so the charity had confidence in my ability. They put me on the Mindfulness-Based Stress Reduction course (MBSR, not the teacher certification course). Maybe there was something I could learn? I realised why I saw some people who had done the MBSR but still believed they could not meditate. That is, until taught by me.

The MBSR framework is useful and works for many people. Yet, there were certain elements I had been introducing to the anxiety group. Elements that can make a huge impact on your practice. Over the years, I'd gained qualifications in several therapies and introduced a couple of tools to the group. That was one, but I was also able to show clear evidence of the benefit of meditation. You can read about the evidence I gathered in chapter 10 (*Myth: Meditation Is Too Difficult*)

Recognising the blessing of having useful insights to share, I set up the new course: teaching highly experienced meditators how to become meditation teachers. It then became crucial to articulate the foundations of meditation. Another three-month retreat, with the guidance of a Tibetan Buddhist Lama and the energetic blessings of a Rinpoche, definitely made its mark. Out of that three-year search, I uncovered the framework.

As part of my spiritual exploration, I attended many Enlightenment Intensives in Bath, UK. Separately, I also qualified in a process to facilitate a satori experience. Just so you know, a satori is generally a foundational level awakening. It is based upon your direct experience, not philosophy, faith, or scripture. There are levels of satori, and the first level isn't necessarily the permanent transformation of *full* awakening, but it tells you enlightenment is true.

All the parts are now in place so I may fulfil my mission – to play my part in the evolution of consciousness. Ninety percent of your personal evolution is a healing journey. Therefore, most of what I do is around making that journey quicker, easier, and more effective.

The IntrAnaut Academy is the vehicle to deliver meditation to you via the app. But what do I mean by IntrAnaut™? Read on to find out.

2

What Is an IntrAnaut?

You may know *astronauts* are passionate about exploring outer space. An intrAnaut is inspired to explore their *inner* space: the vastness of their mind. An intrAnaut is a meditator who has taken their practice to the next level.

On his blog post, *intranaut two-step* (at intranaut.blogspot.com), the author George Breed explains why an intranaut wants to journey into their inner space:

> 1. The inner infinity is as vast as the outer infinity. Our inner world is as vast as the outer world.
>
> 2. The inner infinity and the outer infinity are one infinity. Our inner world and the outer world are one world.
>
> We are the gateway between two infinities. It is only when the gate is closed that we have a problem.

The onslaught of the outer world overruns most people. They feel they have no choice but to put 100% of their focus on that side of their existence. The side we call *reality*.

People do not realise that visiting their inner space will have a powerful effect on how they handle their daily life. Nor do they know meditation can give you a higher vantage point than that experienced by astronauts.

To become a fully qualified intrAnaut, you use all seven ways to meditate.

As an example of how you can use the seven spheres to become an intrAnaut. Get ready to:

1. Build your (inner) space capsule *Restful Absorption (RA)*.

2. Explore deep (inner) space – *Engrossed Attention (EA)*.

3. Make contact with wondrous realms you didn't know existed – *Intentional Awareness (IA)*.

4. Discover your (inner) worlds of authentic emotions – *Authentic Attitudes (AA)*

5. Go beyond your wildest fantasies – *Visualisation or Imagination (VI)*

6. Intuitively find the answers to your questions – *Question or Introspect (QI)*

7. Call upon your highest truths – *Mantra or Invocation (MI)*

The terms in italics are explained in the next chapter (briefly), and there is a chapter for each. By the time you reach the end of the book, you will be able to look back and know how those seven ways to meditate can create an IntrAnaut.

What Do You Want from Meditation?

Most people, myself included, get into meditation to solve a problem.

- My mind is too hyper – never shutting up!

- My body needs healing – I can no longer control how it feels or behaves.

- My emotions are all over the place – anxiety is ruining my life!

- I need to focus and perform better in my sport/job.
- I need to take control of my anger.
- Parts of my body are shutting down.
- I feel helpless and depressed.
- I cannot stop grieving.
- I need to control my stress levels.
- I need to get a handle on my sleep pattern.
- Add yours here ....

For many meditators, their practice takes them further than just the end of their problem. Often the result is a re-wiring that goes beyond success in their goals. Their life is less stressful, but also more fulfilling, happy, and beautiful.

Mindset v Meditation

This re-wiring is a major difference between trying on a new *mindset* and meditation. You attempt a mindset change by thinking new thoughts. Meditation re-wires your brain from beyond the thinking mind. A quick discussion on the left and right brain will show you what this means.

Thinking Left Brain v Intuitive Right Brain

The left brain is logical, practical, and has a worldview based on physical survival: the *thinking* mind. For the left brain, things are separate (them, me, and things), which leads to fear.

The right brain is creative, out-of-the-box, and genius: the *intuitive* mind. For the right brain, experiences are beautiful and connected, and this leads to feelings of love.

Meditation helps your right brain to connect with your left-brain so you may grow holistically. Meditation lifts the lid on your right brain, so you grow in ways that may seem magical.

There are others far more familiar with the L-R brain model and neuroscience than I am. The important point is, there are levels of your mind far beyond your normal *thinking*.

Bottom Line

You have inner resources upon which you should be able to rely. When stressed, it shuts off your connection to those (right brain) resources. Those who have read *Stress, Anxiety & the Battle for Your Sanity* or lived with chronic stress will recognise the following.

Life becomes fearful. This makes it harder for our higher emotions (love, compassion, etc.) to arise easily. When we are in this unsettled state, our immune system is less effective and other bodily systems start to fail.

Meditation can return you to balance.

You may want to get more from life and achieve your greatest potential. You may wonder, "How can I access the intuitive, creative, loving, and joyful parts of myself more easily?" One path is to become a meditator.

This book helps you explore exactly how meditation can do that. Read on to begin your journey by pinning down what meditation is – and is not.

3

What Is Meditation?

A purposeful activity of the mind, with seven principles and making use of the two core, or more, of the seven technologies.

IMAGINE A PRINCE (OR princess) who has never ridden a bicycle before. Today, they want to travel short distances on country roads. These country roads have no cars, but this person of privilege has only ever driven sports cars. Out of range of any internet connection, they receive a bicycle. With no instructions, they believe the pedals are for the brake and drive. Cycling is a non-starter.

Our imaginary future monarch may give up in frustration. Long before they ever gain the thrill of the wind in their hair, the exhilaration of speed, or the glow of perspiration.

Too many times, I've seen new meditators give up in frustration because of incorrect assumptions about the practice. Yes, meditation can be easy – like riding a bike – hmm. Let me ask you a question.

How many forms of meditation are there?

If you ask people to number the types of meditation, how many would say seven? Some people say, "The only way to meditate is...", so for them, the answer is *one*. Others say there are 1000s (e.g., 100s of different mantras).

When people research the meaning of meditation via books (outside the place where they first heard about it), they find many definitions. Some are so broad as to be meaningless (e.g., "A technology of the mind").

Some are very specific and exclude all other forms of meditation. Yet others are plainly incorrect.

The Definition of Meditation

We can split the definitions into two key themes:

1. The essential *components of meditation* practice (I call these the *mind-technologies* used for meditation).

2. A definition that attempts to distil the central *aim* or *benefits of meditation*.

With the first definition, we often see an explanation limited to one type of meditation. To me, a *benefit* or *purpose* of meditation (see the second type of definition above) doesn't tell you anything about what you need to do to meditate. We can use meditation for many *goals* – e.g., to achieve worldly success or de-stress.

The definition used by the Meditation Teacher College:

> Meditation is a purposeful activity of the mind, with seven principles and making use of the core two, or more, of *the seven technologies*.

The definition presented here is broad. Too broad without discussions on the seven spheres of meditation and many other clarifications.

Since meditation is an "activity of the mind", the seven spheres are mind-technologies.

The phrase, *"a purposeful activity"* tells us there is a goal we want to achieve, therefore our meditation is intentional. Being an *activity*, it <u>cannot</u> be *doing nothing*.

The seven mind-technologies/forms/spheres/types, are not the seven principles of meditation.

I decode the seven principles in the book, *7 Secret Codes of Meditation* (to be published in 2023). The principles are not required knowledge for you to get started, but are invaluable for progressing in your practice. I list them in the last chapter.

The Seven Spheres

The seven technologies of meditation (M) are:

Restful Absorption (RA)

Intentional Awareness (IA)

Engrossed Attention (EA)

Authentic Attitudes (AA)

Visualisation or Imagination (VI)

Question or Introspect (QI)

Mantra or Invocation (MI)

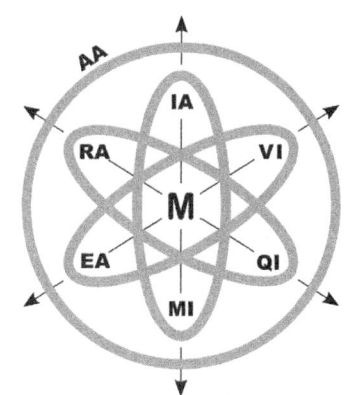

I know you want me to explain exactly what I mean by these terms. There is a chapter devoted to each. The seven spheres are a complete framework with which you can assess your meditation practice. You can then make adjustments for better results.

As the definition says, every meditation will rely on at least the two core mind-technologies, or it is not meditation. The two core spheres are RA and IA. Additionally, you can use any sphere in your meditation: as the main dish or as an ingredient. Below is a quick definition of each of the seven technologies. However, before proceeding, here is a heads-up on a phrase you will see often.

Objects of Meditation

The *object of meditation* is the primary focus of your awareness. The *object* is what you are directing your attention toward, and wanting to know something about it.

For convenience, I'll mention *one* such *object,* although there is a vast array to choose from. Let's say the *object* for your meditation is your breath – *the sensations at the nostrils*. Place your awareness there. You may notice the air going in is a little cooler than the warm air of the out-breath. You may also observe other sensations. These *sensations at the nostrils* (e.g., temperature, pressure) are the *object* of your meditation.

You can see from this example that the *object* (e.g., breathing) can be a process with many parts. Your *object* could be the process of:

- Thinking or emotions.
- Hearing, or any of the five senses.
- Inner change.

The *object* can be:

- A state (e.g., peaceful).
- A quality (e.g., kind).
- A logical conclusion (e.g., I am good).
- Something imagined (moving or static).

In all cases, the *object* is what you intend to be aware of.

The following is a quick orientation and is not the full definition. Just a few key points for each sphere.

Restful Absorption (RA)

Absorption is the same as the effects associated with falling asleep:

> Your awareness draws inward,
> you start to feel cosy, and
> the world outside disappears from your awareness.

Relax until you feel the effects of absorption, then relax some more. I call this shutting off from the outside world into a warm, comfortable space, *the cocoon effect*. It helps your meditations to be pleasant without distractions. The biggest obstacle is falling asleep.

Intentional Awareness (IA)

IA is moment-by-moment conscious awareness. It can be called *bare awareness*, with nothing added. Defined by Rob Nairn as:

> *Knowing what is happening, while it is happening, without preference.* ~ Rob Nairn

Intentional Awareness meditation is a training that emphasises being present with whatever you are aware of. RA and IA together, are the minimum for all meditation. Without them both, you are not meditating, so they are the two core mind-technologies.

Engrossed Attention (EA)

EA meditation is a narrowing (focusing) of your awareness. It uses introspection and memory to steady your focus on one object. It also helps you to relax deeply without falling asleep. When used as a form of meditation, EA steadies your IA (see above) in a narrow-focused attention. "Engrossed" relates to the special relationship this technology has with absorption. However, it is from a different angle than that of RA.

Authentic Attitudes (AA)

The AAs are completely natural attitudes everyone possesses. They include curiosity, being gentle toward yourself, allowing, kindness, and others. You can strengthen an attitude as a meditation, or use them within all your meditations.

Visualisation or Imagination (VI)

You are using your imagination. VI is especially broad in its uses. For instance, you can use VI for healing purposes or better performance (e.g., in sport). VI doesn't have to be visual images in your mind. Find out why in the chapter on VI.

Question or Introspect (QI)

You are contemplating, asking questions, or introspecting. Although this sounds like an analytical thought process, that part of the meditation is minimal. The emphasis is on the opening to intuition. We find this type of meditation within some forms of prayer or insight/wisdom meditations.

Mantra or Invocation (MI)

Within the context of meditation, a mantra is a tone, or set of syllables, that have shown positive effects. An MI is used to invoke specific frequencies within your mind. Depending on your goals and preferences, there are many MI available.

Other Types of Meditation

I'm defining meditation by the mind-technology used. There are other ways to sort meditation into types — e.g., systems, purpose , or categories.

- *Systems* of meditation are groups of mind-technology that were chosen for a specific purpose and given a name.

- To divide meditations into their *purpose* is another option.

- You could class some as healing meditations and others as meditations to help with your focus or lift your spirits. Other *categories* abound.

All these categories, purposes, and systems are called *types of meditation,* but each uses the mind-technologies described within these pages.

The above is just a quick summary of the main points. Each sphere has its own set of subtleties. I'll also give you examples of how to meditate, focusing on each form.

Before getting into all that, I'd like to mention:

The difference between *informal* and *formal meditation* practices. It's important to know when you are not in meditation.

Why terminology is important, and how it can get in the way.

Why knowing about the *myths of meditation* is a wise move.

4

Formal v Informal Practice (and Myths)

W<small>E LOOKED AT THE</small> definition of meditation. Asking if it's the same as something else is important. How is it different from everything else? Not everything can be a form of meditation, otherwise the word is meaningless.

Below, I look at what *is*, and *isn't,* meditation. This knowledge is important for your long-term practice.

More and more things are called meditation. For instance, using a colouring book. Colouring-in can have you fairly still. Just moving your hands and fingers as you relax and focus on the lines and colours. You are paying attention to what you are doing. You're using the core ingredients of meditation.

Yet it's not a meditation. There is no intention to meditate. Even if you think, "Oh, yes, I'm drawing in my *meditation colouring book*, therefore I'm meditating" that doesn't make it a meditation. It is *meditative*.

There are lots of things that are *meditative*. They put you into a similar mental state as meditation at the shallow end. That means they go *toward* meditation, but they're not an actual meditation.

It can prepare you for meditation, because it gets you calm, focused, being mindful, and allows you to rest. Once you've done your *meditative* warm-up, you're in a really excellent state to meditate.

Formal Meditation Practice

Sitting, lying, or standing still and completely focused (as best you can) on your meditation practice is called *formal* meditation.

Of course, when you are in formal meditation, your mind may drift off. You may get completely distracted. But your intention is to stay present with your meditation.

By the way, there's no limit to how long *or short* your meditation must be to label it *formal*.

Informal Practice

We limit meditation to *an activity of the mind.* Otherwise, it should be called something else.

When you are doing other things, you can *partially* use the mind-technologies. This is called *informal* practice, but it is <u>not</u> strictly meditation. The word *informal* (in this context) means it is <u>not</u> a real meditation practice. You're using one or more of the mind-technologies. This has two benefits:

1. You gain extra time in training, so the results of your *formal* practice will be greater.

2. The mind-technologies you are using improve your other activities.

Does this mean you cannot be meditating while doing any other activity?

Doing something else while meditating will be counter-productive to the effectiveness of your practice.

I encourage beginners, those who have a busy mind, or hectic lifestyle, to do *informal* practice. Often before starting a *formal* practice. Many other teachers also do this. It is a start to getting you into a routine.

Informal practice is encouraging because you can see benefits arising from the simple practices. Teachers can forget to say this is not actual meditation. The aim is to gain some training, so when you start *formal* meditation, you are already halfway there.

Meditation in Movement Is an Informal Practice

Many people have several practices they engage in. One of which is meditation. I'd strongly encourage you to keep your formal meditations separate from all other activities. In this way, you'll reap the blissful rewards quicker.

To *blend* meditation with other things will keep you away from the most meaningful rewards. Those benefits are only gained by exploring the *depths* of your mind.

To <u>not</u> *blend* doesn't stop you from doing them back-to-back. You can engage in an activity just before your meditation without a gap between them.

Is it ever okay to meditate while doing something else?

Once you have been meditating for years (or done long retreats) you may be classed as an adept (a qualified IntrAnaut). From moment to moment, an adept can switch between *formal* and *informal* practice. You may add meditation to your daily life in this way, but please note:

1. You intend to have a regular, *formal* meditation practice, distinct from all other activities. To become an adept, your formal practice is essential.

2. Adding mind-technologies to another activity doesn't make it a meditation. The activity becomes an *informal* practice.

3. Some activities are wonderful to do *alongside* your meditation practice (e.g., tai chi, or breathwork). This doesn't turn those supportive activities into

meditation. Even if they are back-to-back with your formal meditation.

An example of the last one (3): yoga teachers will often do a meditation called Yoga Nidra at the end of a class. The physical poses and stretches are ideal for getting your body and mind ready for the meditation.

Walking Meditation Is an Informal Practice

Despite being called meditation, it is an informal practice. Restful Absorption (RA) is a core mind-technology used in *all* meditations. If you are not at rest (quietly still), you are doing informal practice.

Breathing Techniques Are Not Meditation

Breathing techniques use some *control* to keep the breath even. For example, "Breathe in for a count of four; breathe out for a count of eight." There is no *control* in meditation beyond your nudges into meditation. A *nudge* is mostly the intentions you have.

For example. When doing breathing meditation, you may decide to focus your attention on the tummy. You are not controlling the breath. You are simply feeling how the tummy goes in and out. That's a meditation on the breath.

Can you use breathwork, or breath-yoga, or other breathing techniques at the beginning of a meditation?

Absolutely. You can use any technique – including a walk in nature, chi-gong, or dance – to get you into a comfortable state. Anything, so your body and mind are ready to dive deep into meditation. There may be little or no gap between that activity and your meditation.

Mindfulness Confusion

From the above examples, you may see why 90 per cent of mindfulness is not meditation but an informal practice. There are reasons for staying away from the term, mindfulness, within a book that aims to bring you clarity. I'll go into that in the chapter on Intentional Awareness (IA).

The Myths That Stop People Meditating

Everyone carries a bunch of myths with them. To explain, I'm going to ask a question. I want your honest answer, based on your knowledge of life so far.

There is a trick involved. Some will know the answer straight away. Please forgive me for the con. Please make a solid decision: no matter how (or not) you're sure of its correctness.

Have you heard of seagulls? Would you be able to recognise one? Great, let's continue. From the three photos (below), please identify which one is a *Greater Common Seagull*, which one is a *Lesser Common Seagull*, and which is a *Rarely Spotted Seagull*.

Want to know the answer? I didn't think so. You are correct. None are a seagull. There are no species of *seagull*. They are all *gulls* (a category of many species), although I added some spots to one of them. But you will find a majority who believe a species of *seagull* exists.

In fact, one or two people who read this may say, "Everyone knows Seagulls exist!" There lies the problem: because "Everyone knows", therefore it must be true.

Does this misconception matter in everyday life? Not a jot.

Does it matter if you want to categorise bird species? I hope so. Here is a link to spot different species of gull. https://www.wildlifetrusts.org/how-identify/identify-gulls

There are mistaken beliefs about meditation. They stop people starting a practice or gaining all the benefits.

Does it matter that when I say I meditate, some people think I'm being self-indulgent and escaping from reality by emptying my mind using the mantra "Om"? Not in the slightest.

When that person joins my class wanting to learn meditation, it absolutely matters.

Without clear definitions, it is understandable for people to accept half-truths about meditation. There are many urban myths to trip you up.

Between the chapters on the seven spheres, I'll give you the top mistaken beliefs people hold, especially those who say they cannot meditate.

Let's rest before we get into those mistakes and problems. The first way to meditate I explore with students is called Restful Absorption (RA). If you want to reduce your stress overload, this mind-technology is the one to emphasise.

PART TWO - 7 Ways to Meditate

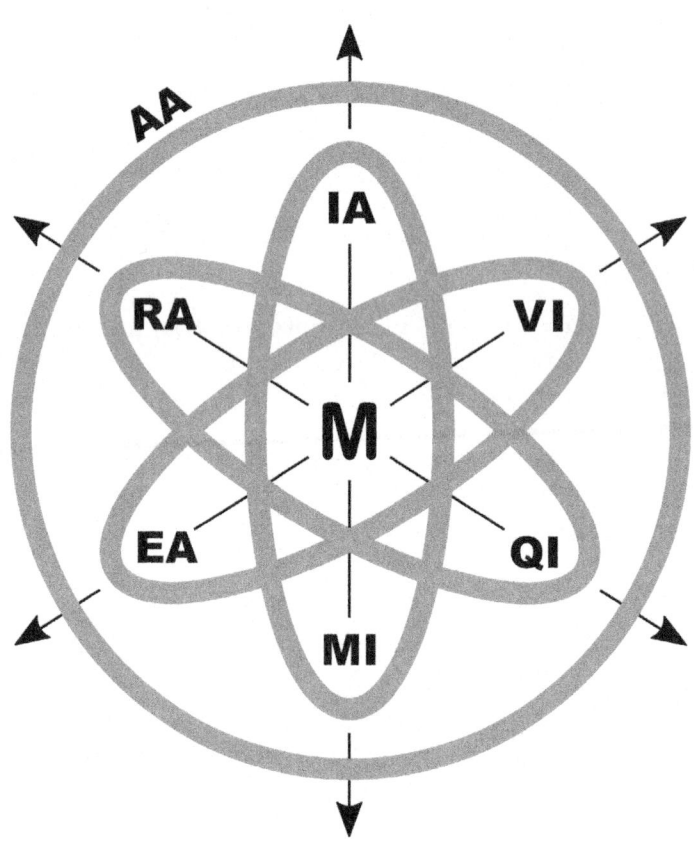

5
Restful Absorption (RA)

SEVEN MIND-TECHNOLOGIES MAKE UP meditation as a whole. The first one we shall explore is Restful Absorption (RA). Along with Intentional Awareness (IA), RA is *core mind-technology* for every genuine meditation.

RA is called *restful* because it is more than just relaxing. People say they can *relax* by having alcohol, slump in front of the TV, or socialising. These are not meditation or the mind-technology of RA. Restful Absorption (RA) goes beyond *trying to relax*.

To rest (instead of struggling to relax), requires gentleness. It is hard to relax if you are being tight, threatening, rough, or controlling. To be gentle can mean being relaxed toward yourself and your practice. Being gentle is one of the Authentic Attitudes (AA), so already we are using more than two mind-technologies.

RA is asking you to be at rest enough for absorption to take effect.

What is absorption? What has it to do with meditation?

Here I'll give you a technical description, plus why it is an essential part of meditation. An easy way to get into this is to discuss how you fall asleep. When you go to sleep each night, you go through a few stages:

1. You turn your mind away from the world outside. Drowsiness can force you to do this.

2. Your body becomes comfortable.

3. Your body becomes less distinct.

4. Your body, and the outside world, disappear from your consciousness completely.

This is your outer conscious awareness being absorbed into your mind. It's like putting a sponge onto a small puddle on the counter. You can watch the sponge absorb the water till there is none left. You could say, your consciousness is being absorbed by drowsiness, until fully immersed in sleep.

The difference between absorption into sleep and absorption when meditating:

- When you fall asleep, you become unconscious (according to some scientists).

- During meditation, you become *more* conscious (of your object of meditation).

This is a crucial difference. The more conscious you are, the more data you have available to you. More data means greater wisdom if you can keep your focus sharp and your mind clear.

This all depends on you staying conscious (as I shall explain in the chapter on Engrossed Attention (EA)) while diving into deeply relaxed states.

Restful Absorption (RA) can be mapped to the four brainwave frequencies (states) as described by science.

Beta 12-30 Hz
Normal awake state

Alpha 8-12 Hz
Relaxed

Theta 4-8 Hz
Deeply relaxed

Delta below 8 Hz
Asleep

When you fall asleep, you are falling through these states, down toward the Delta brainwave pattern (see the image).

It should be noted: all four are active, but one is more prominent. When you're fully awake, there are more Beta waves, so you are in Beta. When resting, or being creative, you're in Alpha but do not totally leave Beta. The volume of Beta waves your brain creates reduces and the Alpha frequency waves increase.

Also, especially if meditating, Theta and Delta will increase but to a smaller extent. When you can calm your mind sufficiently, you will meditate with a prominence of Theta brainwaves. There will be less Beta, some Alpha, and a bit more Delta.

Paraphrasing what I heard from Venerable Kelsang Tharchin, a Tibetan Buddhist monk who is an ex-psychologist:

> You could argue that these various waves are all in the same pond, but with different amounts of disturbance. Whipping up a storm of Beta waves, or settling down to a calm, peaceful, clear pool of Delta waves.

Scientists measuring the brainwaves of Tibetan Buddhist monks also found Gamma waves, which are associated with blissful states. Although beyond this book, we discuss them within the book *7 Secret Codes of Meditation*. Also, look out for my course *Gamma Meditation: Bliss-Out Like A Buddhist Monk* on the app.

Some Benefits of Restful Absorption (RA)

- Absorption is what makes meditation pleasurable (and a huge step closer to blissful and amazing!).

- Absorption is a sign your mind is becoming calm, unfettered by worries.

- RA into Alpha helps with creativity (also known as 'being in the flow/zone').

- RA into Theta and Delta helps with healing and rejuvenation.

- RA (even a small amount) releases stress from the body and mind.

- When your mind becomes calm, through Restful Absorption (RA), you can more effectively connect with your imagination, creativity, and inner wisdom.

There are other spheres of meditation, so the list above only covers a few benefits of meditating. However, these benefits from Restful Absorption (RA), I think you will agree, are significant.

It may take months of meditation before you attain a deep level of Restful Absorption. It is well worth the effort. When you can become more absorbed, your meditations are much more gratifying.

The release of accumulated stress causes suppleness. After months in retreat, I noticed I was able to sit cross-legged (with one foot on my thigh) – without stretching.

Restful Absorption (RA) is highly restorative for your body and mind. Here is a meditation, so you can experience that now.

Meditation: Sleep Yoga – Yoga Nidra

For me, the best part of Yoga was the Yoga Nidra at the end of class. We would lie on our backs on our mats, arms to the sides and feet hip-width apart. By the end of the meditation, I was the one snoring.

Translated as sleep yoga, Yoga Nidra emphasises Restful Absorption (RA). Want to try it?

This is not a full script because I have the audio on the app. If you do not have a smartphone, email me for online access.

1. Get yourself comfortable. Lying is ideal. You could put a pillow under your head and tuck a folded blanket under your knees. A throw placed over you is also a good idea. Check in with your body and mind: do you need anything else? A sip of water? Shut the door? You can't overdo the comfort.

2. Take a deep breath in. As you exhale, feel yourself settling into the comfort you've created for yourself. Remind yourself you cannot fail. You cannot do this wrong. Your experience is perfect, just as it is.

3. Allow yourself to sink into the support beneath you. The embrace of the pillow, blanket under your knees, and firm, warm, steady support beneath; holding you unconditionally. Let go into that unconditional embrace. The body rests cosy and secure. Rest in the comfort, just for you, free and effortless.

4. Intentionally move your awareness to your feet. Check for any tension around your feet, heels, ankles and toes. Become aware of any stiffness, aches or discomfort. With each out-breath, release and let go of any tension. Allow your feet to relax, and to relax fully.

5. When you are ready, bring your awareness to your shins and calves. Check for any tension. Release and let go of any tension you find. Allow your feet to relax, and to relax fully. When ready, move up to your thighs – checking and releasing, relaxing and letting go. Then the same with the pelvic area, lower stomach area and lower back, upper abdominals and middle of your back, your chest and upper back, the shoulders and neck, then the back and sides of the head.

6. Bring your attention to your face. Check for any tension or tightness. Release and let go, relax and soften all the muscles of your face. Soften the forehead on your exhale. Release any tension from the centre of the forehead to the temples. Bring your attention to your brow. Softening, widening across the eyebrows.

Release, let go, and soften.

7. Bring awareness to the jaw. Allow the jaw to drop: relax and soften. The tongue: drop, relax, and soften. Allow the skin and all the muscles of your face to soften and relax. To relax deeply. To relax fully.

8. Back to your shoulders: dropping, softening, relaxing deeply. From the shoulders to the arms, wrists, and hands: softening, relaxing, release and let go. Surrendering to the support.

9. Checking your hands for any tension. Release, let go, and relax, deeply and fully. Check how your hands feel. Do they feel fizzy, fuzzy, or possibly spacious? Do they feel as if they are now mittens, or like cotton wool, or numb but without the pain? This is a sign or absorption.

10. Turn your attention to inside of your body, in the middle. Notice how it feels. If there is a comfortable space or calmness, place your attention inside the space. If there is a pleasant feeling, place your awareness inside any contentment/comfort/bliss. If there is discomfort, release it, let it go, and allow that area to relax fully. Then bring your awareness toward the space, peace, contentment, or calm, and rest in that.

11. Before you get up, turn onto your side. Slowly become aware of your body and surroundings. To become more aware, you may wiggle your toes and fingers; maybe have a stretch. If it's bright, you can put your palms over your eyes for extra gentleness. Allow your eyes to open gently in their own time.

Nuggets

To relax in this way gets you into an absorbed state, similar to falling asleep. As you release stress from your body and mind, it can feel strange, or possibly uncomfortable. Whenever this happens, be attentive (with kindness if you can), and relax the muscles in that area fully. Look out for what I say about *bubbles of stress* (below), because students report it is a useful way to look at what's happening – when rest releases stress.

What about pain?

I have taken mindfulness course students out into a cold wintry night without their coats. I do this to show them a phenomenon I noticed a long time ago.

When outside, I wait a minute while the group tense up to shield themselves from the cold. I ask them to notice the tension. I then get them to relax their muscles and ask them what effect the relaxation has on how cold they feel. They notice the relaxation of the muscles reduces the coldness.

Obviously, with no training, the group tense up again quickly. It is clear, tensing up restricts and somehow *holds on to the cold*. It is the same when we tense up due to pain; the muscles seem to *hold on to the pain*. When we relax, the energy can flow.

When you relax, you are being gentle; no longer constricting, resisting, pushing, or pulling. You give your life-energy a chance to be, move and flow.

Cocoon Effect & Space Capsule

When an astronaut returns and enters the atmosphere, the sky turns blue, and the stars disappear. This is similar to the cocoon effect; the meditators' outer world disappears as they re-enter their homeland. I remember a member of the anxiety group saying that "meditation feels like coming home".

The cocoon effect keeps you in your meditation. It's just you and whatever you're pointing your awareness at. It is like being in the ultimate space capsule.

The cocoon created by Restful Absorption (RA) is your luxury capsule for a voyage to the depths of your mind. It is the reason experienced meditators can sit for an hour (or hours, days, weeks...) with no discomfort.

I should mention, for longer meditations, you need to master Engrossed Attention (EA), to build a superior capsule.

Remember the difference between the cocoon of meditation and falling asleep?

- When falling asleep: drowsiness takes over as you get comfortable and fall into the cocoon of slumber. Your mind becomes dull, then unconscious.

- When meditating: the object of meditation has you engrossed, so you are more conscious as you relax into your cocoon/capsule. The clarity of your awareness becomes sharper.

Most of the sublime benefits of a *long-term* practice come from the cocoon effect. I'm emphasising *long-term* because it can seem as if you can get there quickly if you're drenched in a foggy mind. The chapter on *Attitudes* contains information about a foggy mind.

Release Bubbles of Stress

Next time you are washing the dishes by hand, or bathing in a bath of foamy bubbles, watch as the bubbles burst. Big ones, small ones; sometimes a few splash out of existence in a rush. This is happening to your stress (through absorption) when meditating. Except, you experience it as a big or small *distraction*.

Even with small amounts of absorption, it's as if you release bubbles of deep-seated accumulated stress. These bubbles of stress, when they reach the surface of your awareness, burst. That busting of the bubble, then creates the conditions for a *distraction* – either physical, emotional, or mental.

One way of explaining dreams is to say it is part of your stress-release processes. The dreams may have nothing to do with what was released (although sometimes it may). Neither do the distracting thoughts, emotions, nor physical discomfort when meditating.

Next time you think you've had a terrible meditation (because of all the distracting thoughts) remember the bubbles of stress popping. Celebrate the release of all that stress!

Apart from mental *distractions*, there are also the emotional *distractions*. Since the cause of these emotions are mostly past losses and trauma, your meditation may be uncomfortable at times.

Anxiety, fear, terror, sadness, shame, and any other emotion could enter your meditation. It is important to note: you are *processing* these emotions. The negative emotions from meditation are *shadows* of the things being processed. You can either:

    1. Continue the process by getting back into meditation.

    2. Use other techniques to help you with the processing.

Either way, be gentle and don't focus on the *shadows* created by the processing.

I'd also advise you use RA with several other spheres of meditation to add lots of pleasant feelings to your meditations. I offer a week-long retreat called *Heal With Bliss*, where we *stack the joy* before we do many healing meditations.

Sometimes the distracting thoughts and emotions can be pleasant. When that is the result of a bubble of stress, it is due to a rush of trapped positive energy being released.

RA Is a Secret Code

Rest isn't just a form of meditation or something you only do at the beginning. Rest is one of the secret codes, a *principle* of meditation. Regard it as a *core* of your meditation – from start to finish.

However, if you let go and rest completely right from the start, it can be counter-productive.

There are stages of awareness and experience. You need to refine your intent, depending upon which stage you have attained in your practice. At the beginning, there may be habitual control and a tight focus. Eventually, there must be complete openness and surrender.

On day one of learning to meditate, there may be no mention of *letting go* (unless you do a meditation emphasising Restful Absorption (RA)). Later, it gets mentioned because that pressure you put on yourself can hinder your progress.

The more you meditate, the more relevant RA is to your practice. To comply with the gentleness of RA, we gently nudge. You nudge with a gentle intention.

There is a balancing act between too firm a grip on your meditation or slipping into slumber. It helps if you're getting enough sleep because sleep deprivation will pull you toward slumber.

The good news is, you can use meditation to help you sleep. Just be careful to make it into a definite, intended practice.

> Intend to *let go of the meditation* and *intend to sleep* as soon as you feel the effects of slumber. Make sure you also meditate in ways that do not lead to sleep.

Otherwise, you could find you have created a habit of *meditation = sleep*, which may be difficult to correct.

Stillness

When something is at rest, it is still. Stillness is a core feature of meditation, but some people get the wrong idea. They think if you get an itch, you're not allowed to scratch. That's incorrect.

You don't want to do things that *distract* you. However, if you're itchy or uncomfortable, then you need to move, and that's OK. That's going to help with the remainder of your meditation.

Let me clarify something about stillness and awareness. You're *aware* of your external environment, as well as your internal thoughts and feelings.

Being *intentional in your awareness* doesn't mean looking around externally. If your eyes are moving, you are no longer in *formal* meditation. For meditation, your awareness is engaged, but your body is still. Your mind could be active in imagining, but your body is still.

Silence

If your ears are seeking sounds, then you are no longer in *formal* meditation.

The silence is also about the mind's activities. Allow everything outside to quieten as you focus your attention on your specific practice. Focusing (Engrossed Attention (EA)) helps create the cocoon, which helps you to ignore the sounds from outside.

Restful Absorption (RA) helps your body to rest in stillness, which helps your mind to quieten and rest.

Restful Absorption (RA) sounds a bit like doing nothing, or being self-indulgent. Let's put that myth to rest.

6

Myth: I Cannot Meditate

THERE ARE MISTAKES PEOPLE make about meditation that stop them from gaining all the benefits. Let us look at what stops people from trying (or stop trying).

Meditation Is Doing Nothing, or Indulgent

Restful Absorption (RA) is about relaxing and letting go of control or doing stuff. Surely, that means doing nothing? Is that not a self-indulgent waste of time?

Certainly, those whose attitude is "I'll sleep when I die" will not like the sound of meditation. Scientists tell us if you do not rest in stillness for a few hours (sleep), you go crazy, then become ill and die. A proper amount of sleep is an indicator of a long and healthy life.

This isn't a critique of anyone's lifestyle. It's about the value of rest. When you relax, your brainwaves change, as I describe in the previous chapter. The more you rest, the more the cocoon effect manifests, with its associated benefits. Instead of seeing it as doing nothing, you could view Restful Absorption (RA) as a way to build your space-capsule.

With a well-built meditation capsule, you can explore the vast space of your mind. You become an intrAnaut – a pioneer of the last frontier. We cannot say a pioneer is doing nothing.

Is meditation self-indulgent? This depends on the goal you have for your meditation practice. When I was a newbie, I often listened to guided meditations just for the enjoyment. They lifted me out of whatever slump I was in. I would meditate for the entertainment value.

You could say, at that point, my meditations were self-indulgent. In hindsight, those *self-indulgent* meditations started me on the road to many insights. Even if they would not get me to the deeper realisations, they were great training. Some were therapeutic.

I Cannot Empty My Mind

Almost daily, I meet people who say they cannot empty their mind, or believe this is the purpose of meditation. You may have heard this one yourself.

At one time, I thought "The purpose of meditation is to stop my incessant thinking". I had an abundance of thoughts that never shut up. This led me to believe there was no way I can achieve any calmness of mind. I tried – unsuccessfully – to subdue my thoughts; proving I am unable to meditate. I was ready to give up.

During the meditation classes, I listened carefully. The teacher said "Watch your thoughts pass by like bubbles". My attempts to visualise my thoughts as bubbles had me daydreaming of balloons. On discussing my plight with the meditation teacher, I found my first nugget.

> The thoughts are allowed to be there. You are simply asked not to involve yourself with them. Emptying the mind or stopping one's thoughts is probably the number one myth about meditation.

Now the challenge is to *let go of being enmeshed* in my thoughts!

Meditating on the breath is supposed to be easy. The instructions were to observe the sensations in the nostrils, throughout the whole breath. Be mindful of distracting thoughts and bring your awareness back to the breath. Why couldn't I make my meditation work?

With a goal-achieving mindset, I sat diligently – for hours – only to be met with frustration at the lack of progress. Once I realised I was thinking, I'd push and pull the breath to perceive the sensations.

I noticed I could stay in contact with the breath for longer if I controlled the breath and focussed hard to keep my awareness steady. My brow tightened, and I felt a squeeze around my head like a rubber band. Headaches became a regular visitor to my meditations.

Once in a while, I'd be rewarded with calmness during my sit. The inner peace was glorious, so I didn't want this heaven to fade. I'd try to hold on to the tranquillity in the same way as the sensations of the breath. Another head-pounding ensued. It was a challenge to relax and let go.

I was told to:

> Take away the emphasis on calming and stopping your thoughts. To untangle yourself from your thoughts means to – as best you can – ignore them. Trying to push them away is counter-productive. Far better to let them be and focus your attention on your breath.
> Your focus, however, mustn't be too rigid. Remember, the instruction at the beginning of each meditation is to relax. This emphasis on relaxation isn't just for the beginning, but for the whole meditation.

It wasn't as if I hadn't been told any of this before. What made me miss those vital nuggets of wisdom? It may have been a wish to get it right.

The principles of success you heard about in school, college, and work do **not** apply to meditation. Goal setting, resilience, and pushing through may help you progress in life. In meditation, they are more likely to impede your progress.

Throughout this book, you'll find the answers to my questions and what I've worked out since then.

The Seduction of a Blank Mind

To have an empty or *blank mind* is not the intention or purpose of meditation. Nor what it does. Meditators can, however, fall into a half-asleep state. Many people have been taught the cocoon effect of sleepiness is meditation. That's incorrect. It can be very inviting, blissfully peaceful, and cosy within the cocoon of slumber. It's easy to fall into, but we need to be diligent.

Once we make that half-asleep state into a habit, it's hard to remedy.

You now know how **not** to meditate.

- Don't try to empty your mind.

- Don't *try* to relax; or use control, force, or willpower, to make your meditation fit your thoughts of how it should be.

- Don't mistake the blankness of slumber for meditation.

Through knowing not only *what* to do, but *why* each nuance of the practice is important, you can experience all that meditation can offer.

7
Intentional Awareness (IA)

MEDITATION IS *OF THE* mind. Many people do not realise their *awareness is part of their mind*. They think their mind is only the thoughts in their head.

The nun sat on a chair on stage, resplendent in her clean burgundy red robes with a streak of golden yellow to show her lineage of Tibetan Buddhism. She said, "Check if you are breathing." Moments went by as we looked at each other. Meanwhile, I noticed an irritation at being asked to focus on a bodily function obviously happening because I'm alive.

She continued, "Make sure you are actually breathing." Relenting, and after a moment of struggle to apprehend my breath, I paid attention to the movement of my chest. "You are now meditating." Pardon?

She explained that *intentional awareness is a form of meditation*.

Along with Restful Absorption (RA), IA is a core mind-technology in *every* meditation. It is the part that helps you be more conscious as you meditate.

IA meditation has these components:

- Being present – which cannot be anywhere else but in the here and now.

- Paying attention without the need to think. You will notice what's happening, but without getting involved with analysing or evaluating. You may notice your mind analyses and evaluates, but you ignore it.

- Your intentions dictate the purpose of your Intentional Awareness (IA).

Most mindfulness teachers say mindfulness must also be non-judgemental. For me, that puts too much pressure on those who have chronic anxiety.

Some are likely to say, "I cannot stop my mind from judging all the time, therefore I cannot meditate." Within the framework you are holding in your hands, a non-judgemental attitude is not a prerequisite to engage in your (IA) practice.

You are *encouraged* (but not required) to cultivate a neutral mind (neither positive nor negative). The neutral mind is a part of the Authentic Attitudes (AA). The AAs help your Intentional Awareness (IA) become a source of positive change in your life.

You are (working toward the ideal of) not labelling, or judging, or assuming, or getting involved with anything. You are simply *with* your experience. Being interested (another AA) in your raw experience will help you sustain your IA.

Intentional Awareness (IA) at its root is *to notice on purpose*: to know what is happening. Knowing depends on awareness.

Try this Body Scan meditation to experiment with this idea.

Meditation: Body Scan

For this meditation, you pause in each area to pay attention to what presents itself. You may find places where it is hard to detect anything. That's OK, because you are still *noticing* your awareness seems dull in that area of your body. Nothing to worry about. Most people have that in their experience. By engaging in a regular practice, the numbness dissipates so you can feel into all areas of your body.

This meditation takes your Intentional Awareness (IA) to all parts of your body.

1. Get yourself comfortable. Sit, stand, or lie down.

2. Intentionally focus on your feet.

3. Feel your toes, heels, ankles and soles of your feet. Notice the tactile sensations. Be aware of any pressure from your footwear. What is the temperature: cool, warm, or hot in places? What does it feel like inside the foot?

4. Despite the questions as prompts, you are not looking for thoughts about it. Simply being aware of the sensations.

5. Know that you are paying attention. You don't need to think to be aware (even if thoughts arise as well).

6. Bring your focus to your shins and calves. Detect (with your awareness, not thinking) what you can about the experience of your calves and shins. Both outside and in. Allow any thoughts to be there, but pay more attention to your physical awareness.

7. Go through your body in any order you wish: include all parts of the front, back, sides, arms and head.

Nuggets

You may notice your mind is analysing, comparing, or narrating. All that is OK; it's what the thinking mind does. No need to push it away, or try to stop thinking.

At best, you will drop your involvement with the thinking (while the mind carries on *doing its thing*). Being conscious of what is happening for a few moments is great. You may notice when you turn your awareness toward your thoughts, they often become shy and quiet.

There is nothing within Intentional Awareness (IA) that says your meditation should be pleasant, or peaceful. In fact, you are likely to become aware of uncomfortable feelings, sensations, or thoughts. Meditation doesn't have to *feel* a certain way. An uncomfortable feeling, sensation, or thought, simply means there is stress to be released.

Further on in the book, you will find out about the Authentic Attitudes (AA). These *Attitudes,* such as the *Beginner's Mind,* and *Gentleness,* help to safeguard your peace and sanity. They are an antidote to our tendency to create more stress.

When you combine the *Inner Smile* meditation (within the chapter for AA) with the Body Scan (above), you have a highly therapeutic meditation. This combination will also transform your relationship with your body.

For now, know that the Authentic Attitudes (AA) help meditation become easier. You'll learn how simple the instructions are in a few chapters from now.

The Ability to Know

With Intentional Awareness (IA), there is the ability to know. The *Principle of Intent* – as described in the book, *7 Secret Codes of Meditation* – tells us the essence of your being wants to know. You want to be fully conscious. Awareness is knowing.

You can check this out by being aware of different parts of the body, and finding a part that feels different from what you expected. For instance, there may be an ache in the back or a tickle on a foot. You can ask, "How do I know about the tickle?", or "How do I know about the ache?" Well, the reason you know is because you are aware of it.

This section is for those who've heard about *mindfulness*. It's of greatest interest to those who're wondering why I've not called IA, *mindfulness*. This next section is also for those who've learnt meditation from a tradition, but IA *doesn't* describe what you know as mindfulness.

If you do not need a discussion on why I'm avoiding the term *mindfulness*, skip to the next chapter.

Mindfulness Has Three Different Meanings

There are more than three definitions, but these are the main (authoritative) ones from Buddhism.

1. Secular mindfulness teachers and some Theravada Buddhists use a definition similar to:

> Mindfulness is the awareness that emerges through paying attention on purpose, in the present moment, and non-judgementally, to things as they are. ~ Williams, Teasdale, Segal, and Kabit-Zinn (2007)

It's your *bare awareness* you are engaging, or being present with (without additions, such as opinions or thoughts). In my framework, this is Intentional Awareness (IA).

2. From a Tibetan Buddhism perspective:

> *Mindfulness refers to attending continuously to a familiar object, without forgetfulness or distraction.*

You are <u>not</u> *being distracted,* because you are remembering to stick with the *familiar* object of your meditation. A *familiar object*, is one you've already given some attention (see Objects of Meditation in Chapter 3 for more on what an *object* is). Engrossed Attention (EA) in my framework.

3. A teacher of Theravada Buddhism once said:

> *Mindfulness is the faculty that notices that distraction has occurred and redirects the attention.*

They use the analogy of a raven that is set free from a ship – before modern navigation systems. The bird flies high and circles in all directions. It is looking for land, watched by the crew. In Tibetan Buddhism, this faculty is called *introspection*. Notice this faculty only kicks in *after* you have been distracted. As you may have guessed, this is the mind-technology I call Question or Introspect (QI).

From outside the various Buddhist traditions, there appears to be confusion about the term *mindfulness*. But there's no confusion if you are within one of those traditions. With rare exceptions, their explanations are far more complete than any framework presented by secular mindfulness teachers.

The terms I am using (IA, EA, QI, etc.) are the framework outlined for the Meditation Teacher College, not any one tradition.

It doesn't matter which definition of mindfulness they have taught you. The important thing is: to cover the ideas for those *three* definitions. With that knowledge, you know what is happening and why. It is also vital that the terms are consistent within the framework.

The framework presented here is not meant to replace the traditions. It's an explanation for those who have no intention of joining a tradition. To help you, there is also a Glossary at the end of the book.

Back to the three mind-technologies described by Vipassana teachers, Tibetan scholars, and others. Here is how my framework describes them:

> 1. **Intentional Awareness** (IA) is an observation of what is available to your awareness. In some Theravada

Buddhist traditions, and mindfulness teachers outside of Buddhism, IA is *mindfulness*. Whatever arises within your awareness is a good candidate for IA. This mind-technology lets you know what's there, right in front of you.

2. **Engrossed Attention** (EA) is a reply to your wish to know more deeply. When your meditation focus is narrow (EA), the details become more distinct. It *remembers your intention* and steadies the awareness. EA equates to *concentration meditation* from some Theravada Buddhist traditions – but you don't concentrate on anything. EA is called *mindfulness* in Tibetan Buddhist traditions.

3. **Question or Introspect** (QI) asks questions for a deeper understanding. Introspection also acts as a guide for staying within your meditation – like the raven analogy above. Some Theravada Buddhists say this is a part of *mindfulness*. Tibetan Buddhists tell us it is *introspection*.

All three mind-technologies work together during most meditations.

There is a diagram over on the next page to help you see how this works. As you look at this page, you have the intention to understand.

When you intend to know clearly, your mind focuses on the page with Engrossed Attention (EA). Your intention keeps you focussed (EA).

At first, you are vaguely aware of your environment, because the space of your Intentional Awareness (IA) is larger than the object.

When you have the intention to know clearly (or more deeply), your mind focuses on the object with Engrossed Attention (EA)

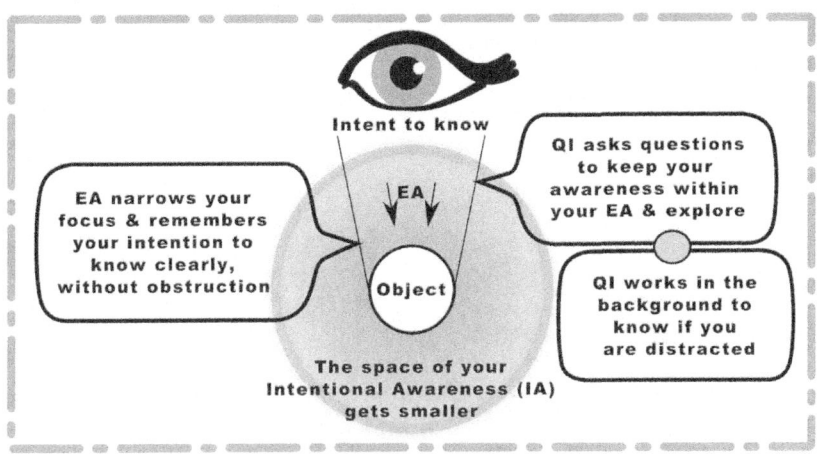

- Intent to know
- EA narrows your focus & remembers your intention to know clearly, without obstruction
- QI asks questions to keep your awareness within your EA & explore
- QI works in the background to know if you are distracted
- The space of your Intentional Awareness (IA) gets smaller

EA narrows your focus and remembers your intent to know clearly. Meanwhile, Question or Introspect (QI) works in the background to ask if you are distracted.

All these different parts of meditation can make it appear complex. No wonder teachers want to give us the simple version.

There are reasons people can believe meditation is too difficult. Have a rest while you read about the myth that you have to try hard to succeed in meditation.

8

Myth: Try Hard to Succeed

WHAT DOES IT MEAN *to try too hard?*

- Trying too hard is about control. You're trying to control the outcome, or your experience.

- Trying too hard creates distractions. By pushing, we create the internal environment – or tightness – for distractions to happen.

Imagine a small child. You gently throw the child a huge beach ball, but it bounces off them. Funny, but not so much for the child. Switching to a better size of ball, you try again. This time, their grip is not tight enough, so it slips out of their hands.

Next time, they grip it tightly, and are rewarded with the success of a catch.

In adulthood, they know how to catch. What if you throw the first ball they caught as a child to this adult? But this time you cover it in the slipperiest of oil? The vice-like grip they used as a child, and has worked well for them ever since, would have the ball slip away. Not enough grip and it slips through.

If it is you with the ball, it wouldn't take a minute to figure out the right amount of pressure to hold the oily ball. It is not so easy to know how much pressure you need within meditation.

There needs to be some effort, but people grip too tightly. Treating your practice as if it were a greasy ball may help to loosen your grip without slipping off.

Adjustments will need to be made. The more altitude you gain in meditation, the less effort you need (see the Nuggets section in the next chapter for *"How will I know I am engrossed?"*)

How to Try Too Hard

In meditation, you try to:

- Get it right by staying in control. You're controlling, pushing, or pulling. For example (in a breath meditation), if you are forcing the breath out a little, to feel the sensations.

- Keep excellent contact with the breath.

- Hold on once you have contact. Maybe you experience a lovely, peaceful state and want to hold on to it. This one can be subtle.

- Stop yourself from being distracted. You try to make your meditation work!

- *Create* a visualisation instead of *allowing them to emerge.*

- Contemplate or visualise a complex topic.

- Impose quiet on your mind. It just creates stress. Let's hope you're not trying to empty your mind or stop thinking. Your thoughts are allowed to be there. They are not the enemy.

- Be goal-oriented in and between sessions, so there is not enough rest. A goal-achieving mindset is detrimental to your practice. Therefore, people who are driven can have a hard-time with their meditation.

The answer is, "Don't do it!"

The more often (and the more of them) you engage in, it's highly likely you're creating the conditions for the very severe consequences outlined below.

On my Facebook profile, I once had a cartoon of a young monk. The thought bubble said, "Come on enlightenment, I haven't got all day!" If you are driven, have a goal-setting mindset, are ambitious, or want to get it right; you are probably trying too hard.

Effects of Trying Too Hard

We can explain the effects of trying too hard in various ways. For example, if you are focusing too hard, you may get a headache. It can feel like a tight rubber band around your head at the brow.

Headaches have various causes. Definitely make sure you drink enough water before meditation, because dehydration can be a cause of headaches.

If you get headaches outside meditation, then trying too hard in meditation will probably worsen the problem. A headache during meditation could also be a sign you're also trying too hard outside meditation.

Possibly, you could have a tightness or a sharp pain in your chest. With this one, get it checked out for any potential physical cause. It may become stronger when you meditate and be accompanied by:

- A highly distracted mind (not just a blip because of current stress).

- An inability to focus in and out of meditation.

- Emotional sensitivity.

According to Tibetan Buddhism, derived from India, these effects are the by-product of energy imbalances. There are also many other ways these energy imbalances can manifest.

Modern medicine will have its own explanations (but maybe not). The important thing is, the symptoms are real, and we know the cause – trying too hard.

People can have these symptoms prior to seeking the benefits of meditation.

How to Remedy Trying Too Hard

The imbalance is not a physical cause and effect (check with a medical professional to make sure). The imbalance is not from a mental cause, although there are mental distortions created by the imbalance.

My best explanation? It is an emotional (or energetic) imbalance, which affects the body and mind. This is why talking therapies (although useful on issues within the mental arena) have a limited effect on these types of imbalances.

If you are reading this, having already found yourself with the symptoms detailed, you may need professional help. I offer retreats and 1-on-1 coaching to support people out of the pit of despair these symptoms cause. Meanwhile, use these suggestions to help gain some balance.

1. Stop all complex meditations. Stop any meditation that you find is aggravating the symptoms. Not forever: just while you use other techniques to bring you back to balance.

2. Get grounded. Connect with the earth as much as possible:

   - Gardening, walk in nature, hug a tree, or do pottery.

   - Lie on the ground to rest or meditate.

   - Emphasise Restful Absorption (RA) type meditations after stacking joy (see Stacking Joy on the app).

   - Laughter Yoga and Hugging Workshops.

- Sex (not Tantra).

- Eat root vegetables, raw vegetables and fruits, and plenty of protein foods (including meat if allowed).

- Give yourself special time for your emotions to vent.

- Inner Child practices (not just visualisation), or Ho'oponopono.

- Breathwork.

Use the mobile app to find practitioners who specialise in the remedies mentioned, and others.

Process or Training?

In some meditation schools, they talk about *training the mind*. I find the word *process* fits better. It's not as if you are on a training course to get a certificate for taking copious notes.

Although there are skills you can develop, meditation is mostly about applying the process.

As a process, you do not have to worry about achieving the goal (this creates stress). Instead, your goal is to meditate (without expectations) and meditate some more. You are giving your mind and body the chance to heal your stress. This healing leads to experiencing peaceful states (but not all the time).

Why is this process distinction Important?

In the West, they brought us up to believe we can achieve anything as long as we try hard enough. *"Working hard and pushing ourselves is the key to success!"* is the message we get about making gains in almost any endeavour. But for meditation, these same attitudes are dangerous!

I liken it to playing a game of snakes and ladders.

It may seem that you're climbing the ladder of success with your meditation (for a little while). However, you *shall* land on a snake and feel as if you are back at the beginning.

Some days you are up. Then, for no apparent reason, you are struggling to find the peace you expect. This process is entirely natural.

On the days when your meditation sucks, it gives you a chance to train in patience. You can be gentle with yourself and use Intentional Awareness (IA). Plus, relax into the tension created by expectation.

How do I do the process?

With a gentle nudge, you get yourself into the process without pushing or pulling. The only effort is to:

Persist in getting into the routine of scheduling your meditation, then sitting to do it.

Persevere in finding your object of meditation. Then when you drop it, to find it again. When your Engrossed Attention (EA) meditation becomes more refined, you will need only a nudge to continue to keep the object of meditation clear.

Have the discipline to intentionally use the mind-technologies while mindful of the Authentic Attitudes (AA). The gentle nudge.

Be observant and curious enough to spot when you are getting tight, pulling, or pushing, so you can rest instead (not resist).

Be attentive to how conscious you are. In meditation, you become more consciously aware. If your cocoon takes you into a cosy slumber, then you are being taken away from meditation.

That tightrope walk, between control and slumber, is the training part of meditation. You are training yourself to discern the difference. However, meditation isn't something with which you can use goal setting. Authoritative, step-by-step instructions are crucial to getting you into meditation. But once you're meditating, you need to allow the process to do its thing.

Within individual meditations, there are signs of absorption (RA) you can recognise. You get there through the process of releasing stress and the training in discernment. In retreat, you can identify milestones or stages, which show you are on the right track for definite attainments. But we gain these through the process produced by specific meditations.

What's the difference between a nudge and trying too hard?

With a nudge, you gently apply the guidance given, with as little control as possible. To help you identify this more clearly, use the *Intent – Let Go* technique as described in Chapter 21 under, Nurture Your Practice (4).

Be curious about the amount of control you apply. How much can you let go, yet still have a glimpse of contact with your meditation? If your awareness drifts, this is because of a bubble of stress being released, or you've let go of your intent. Without fuss, gently nudge your awareness back to the meditation.

Achieve or Attain?

We *achieve* by trying hard to reach a goal (a measurable benefit).

We *attain* because of running a *process* until a measurable benefit is obvious.

The effort involved in meditation is only to keep the process going. This has the side-effect of training the mind to be focused and mindful. That's what makes meditation a powerful tool so you can have more control over your life. Again, making these things into more than a long-term goal/attainment (which will manifest when enough processing in meditation has been done) will be counter-productive.

You <u>must not</u> try hard, push yourself, or try to achieve a clear mind for as long as you can during meditation! I know this from my personal experience.

With a regular practice, you gain an increased ability to be aware of the changes. One type of meditation that helps hugely with developing this ability is Engrossed Attention (EA).

Continue reading to discover the secret practice everyone knows about but few master.

9
Engrossed Attention (EA)

You could say, Engrossed Attention (EA) is a specialised form of Intentional Awareness (IA).

Paying attention to various objects in a sequence (e.g., body parts) comes under the banner of Intentional Awareness (IA). That's because you are not intending to stay with one thing for long.

When you intend to stick around and observe just one object (e.g., the breath), you are using Engrossed Attention (EA).

You could argue that EA is being used for each of the body parts in the IA meditation. That's correct and shows how IA and EA work together whenever you focus your attention. But Engrossed Attention (EA) is more than just purposefully paying attention to whatever arises.

Before continuing with an explanation of EA, I'd like to recommend an *object of meditation* (also see Objects of Meditation in Chapter 3 for more on what an *object* is).

EA Objects of Meditation

The *object* can be almost anything, but at the end of this chapter, I tell you why using a candle is not the best.

I recommend the sensations associated with the breath – either at the tummy or the entrance to (or inside) the nostrils. If you cannot use the nostrils, then use the belly (i.e., at the stomach; it is the feeling of the abdomen rising and falling).

As you do the breathing meditation and become more focused on the sensations of your breath, you are also becoming engrossed. The process includes:

1. Bring your awareness to the object (the breath).

2. You notice your mind has wandered to something else (thoughts, other body sensations, sounds, etc.).

3. You bring your awareness back to the object (the breath).

Now, let's look at EA in more detail.

Engrossed Attention (EA) Keeps Your Awareness Steady

If you hold a powerful telescope in your hands, the image through the lens will be unclear. With EA training, it is as if we hold the telescope on a tripod. Therefore, we gain clarity by having a solid stand (training in EA).

In meditation, short-term memory is a function of EA. You point your awareness and then the functioning of memory within EA helps you stay attentive.

Have you ever read a book on a train or bus and missed your stop? If so, you may understand how, when you focus your attention on something of interest, the world can go by without you noticing.

People get so engrossed in a movie that they jump at the scene made to shock you or cry at the sad scenes. You maybe engrossed in this exciting read!? When engrossed, you notice little of what is happening around you.

The same phenomenon can occur when you are with someone and give them your full attention. Everything falls away into the background of your awareness while you focus on them and what they are saying.

Becoming engrossed also happens when you get engrossed in worries, anger, or fearful thoughts!

Engrossed Attention (EA) helps us to know the detail. Imagine you have a painting of a landscape. You can see the colours and shapes, but what about the detail?

This is where narrowing your focus of attention comes in. Maybe noticing the brushstrokes or noticing how the lamp behind you shines on a particular part of the painting. That's focused knowing.

It's the part that knows the details through a finer and finer degree of focus. This concentrated focus is why this type of meditation is sometimes called *concentration meditation*, or *single-pointed meditation*.

I don't like those terms because I took them to heart and messed up my meditation. The *concentration* is not what you do, but a result of becoming engrossed in the details.

Engrossed or Absorbed?

There is a relationship between Engrossed Attention (EA) and Restful Absorption (RA). Using RA, you fall through the brainwave frequencies toward Delta (and an ultra-calm mind). In EA, your focus helps you dive deep into the details, creating more conscious awareness. They both induce the cocoon effect – where the rest of the world disappears. Only RA makes the cocoon comfortable and pleasant.

> EA *without* RA, will make your meditation into a tyrannical, controlling monster that will destroy you.

Have I said that strongly enough? If meditation has damaged anyone, then it is because they did what I did. In the previous chapter, I discuss the mistake of *trying too hard*. Make sure you read that, so you will not end up like I did.

Engrossed Attention Helps Restful Absorption and Vice Versa

You activate the EA side of absorption by focusing on one thing. This adds the following characteristics to Restful Absorption (RA):

- Things outside of your focus fade into the background.

- The object of your attention is clearer as you notice more about it.

- The object of your focus appears to get bigger or closer.

- It gets harder to draw yourself away from the object of your focus.

- Unless the object is exciting, your body and mind relax, so your brainwaves also change.

Why the Breath?

The breath is the perfect meditation object.

- You carry it everywhere. You do not need a pocket to keep it in. There is nothing to set up to get the use of it.

- You always have it with you, and it takes less than one second to start.

- You don't need batteries or electricity. It costs nothing and is easy to use.

- Immediately accessible at all times – even if in bed – or with other people.

- Discreet – no one has to know you are meditating.

- The breath has the benefit of being rhythmic and naturally calming if you focus on it. It is neutral (not exciting).

- It also changes continuously, making it more interesting to watch than a brick or spot on the wall.

- It reduces stress and is safe.

EA meditation on the breath can take you toward sublime states. Before you get there, it can calm your mind, release stress, and create an environment within you for contentment.

What Does EA Do?

You are *training your memory* so you can focus on one thing for longer. By having a clear *intention to remember* what you are doing, you are engaging with this practice in a way that is beneficial. The *intention* to *stay in contact* will create tension. This is subtle.

Your essence wants to know, so your questions are things like, "What is happening here? What's the truth? What details are there to uncover?" Your intention is to remember what you are doing. Which is: you are pointing your awareness at the *object* to *know* more about it.

Yes, it would be easier to force your will upon your focus and stick to your object with determination. But that's <u>not</u> meditation. Thankfully, after a few rounds of distraction, your mind starts to stick with your object without any force. If it doesn't, then you are releasing stress. Either use an informal practice designed to release stress, or be gentle on yourself while EA helps your RA to release stress. RA with EA, produces a greater reduction in accumulated stress than RA alone.

Engrossed Attention (EA) breathing meditation is a natural invite to Restful Absorption (RA) to relax your body. This helps to create the cocoon effect. It also reduces the amount of thinking swirling around your head. It gives you a breather if you are dealing with hectic thoughts.

It creates a good internal environment for any other meditation.

There is an analogy often used to describe this supportive inner environment:

1. Imagine a pond, pool, or bowl of muddy water. The silt swirls up because of turbulence. This is a bit like the mind when it keeps churning up more and more stuff for you to think about.

2. Then the wind and rain and swishing of the bowl stop. Analogous to the RA plus EA parts of the meditation having an effect.

3. The silt and mud settle down to the bottom of the pond/pool/bowl, leaving clear water you can see through. You can now see the beautifully coloured fish that were hidden but are now clearly visible.

Once you have reduced the turbulence in your head, meditation becomes a lot easier. You are less likely to get involved and identify with every thought.

With fewer thoughts to deal with, you are in a better position to engage the Authentic Attitudes (AA) (e.g., allowing, and being curious about the remaining thoughts). You don't need to argue (with yourself) for a more positive stance (your mind's opinions battling against its other viewpoints).

Distractions Are Inevitable

Your awareness may drift away from your intended *object of meditation* (e.g., the breath). Most people get distracted quickly and frequently at first. Anything that takes your awareness *completely* away from your object is a distraction. There are two levels of distraction:

1. Your *object* is in the background, but you're still aware of it. Maybe you're more interested in something else, or a part of your mind seems to be. Your mind has *wandered*, but not completely.

2. The object of meditation is no longer within your awareness. You forgot your intention and are now involved with something else. You are *distracted*.

When meditation releases tension, it is analogous to a bubble of stress rising to the surface of your mind/body and popping (releasing). When it pops, your thoughts may wander, or your body twitch/itch, etc. There could be an emotional feeling, or your awareness may stray onto outside things (e.g., noises).

At the beginning of our meditation journey, we all carry heaps of accumulated stress – which needs to be released. We also have little training is EA, so our mind isn't trained to "stay" with the *object* of meditation.

You cannot train a dog to "Stay" by having a session a month. In the same way, it is best to have a regular (optimally, daily) EA meditation session. A regular EA meditation will also help you release enough stress so you're <u>not distracted as much</u> – woohoo!

What if you do <u>not</u> get distracted?

Sometimes a person can say "I do not get distracted by the mind." This can happen when a person has a foggy brain due to stress. A foggy mind is one way stress can affect a person. See the diagram and explanation via the chapter on Attitudes.

It is introspection (Question or Introspect (QI)) that brings your awareness back once distracted. QI does this in the background by asking questions in line with your intentions. These questions ask if you are still remembering to be with your object, and nudge you to notice when the answer is no.

No Time to Meditate?

If you believe you do not have time to meditate, I have a chapter for you, *Myth: I Don't Have Enough Time To Meditate*. But here is something to consider now.

On the first day of the course, Meditation: ABC, I ask students, "What is the minimum time you need to meditate?" I conduct a poll. "Does it take one hour? Thirty minutes? Twenty minutes? Ten, five, three, two, one minute? Thirty seconds anyone?"

You can meditate in less time than it takes for one breath. For people who are busy, or have a busy mind, or just starting with meditation, the One Breath meditation is a great place to start.

Meditation: One Breath

Once you decide to meditate and can feel yourself breathing at the tummy, you are already meditating. If you choose to focus on the sensations at the nostrils, you can observe the cooler air going in and the warmer air going out. Possibly, the different pressure of the exhale compared to the pressure of the air going in.

You don't need to be sitting or lying down. You could stand or be walking or taking a moment at the computer. If walking, you cannot put your full, undivided attention on the breath, but you can do some informal training. It makes it easier for when you can stop. You will also benefit from calming the mind.

Once you establish contact (with the sensations at the nostrils or movement of the tummy), direct your effort gently toward *remembering* to maintain contact. If using the tummy as your contact point, you can place a hand there to help you feel the movement.

Yes, you can meditate in less time than it takes for one breath. This is how:

1. Get yourself comfortable. Maybe sitting on a chair, standing still, or lying down.

2. Bring your attention to your breath. It doesn't matter where you notice the breath. Notice any tactile sensations that confirm you are breathing. It could be the sound of the breath is most prominent: that's OK, pay attention to that.

3. You may be aware of other things as well as the breath. That's OK. Your intention is to be aware of the breath. Anything extra is to be treated as background noise, even if it appears to be up front. You are meditating.

4. Know, consciously, you are being aware of the breath. You are definitely meditating now.

5. [Optional] Be curious about any sensations you may detect (e.g., warm, cool, pressure, or gaps between breaths?). Be open to discovering something new. Make sure you are not unwittingly controlling the breath in order to feel more.

6. Stay aware of the breath for a full inhale and exhale. It may fade in and out of your focus. That's OK.

7. If you have time, you can observe yourself breathe for another One Breath meditation.

When you meditate on the breath, you may notice:

- The sensations in the nostrils (e.g., coolness or warmth, pressures, etc.). Or the rise and fall of the tummy.

- Any gaps between breaths. Changes in the length, or depth, of the breath.

- When you are no longer staying with the sensations (distracted).

- When you can feel the sensations but other things are attractive to your mind at the same time (wandering).

Nuggets

The One Breath meditation facilitates calmness. Even if it feels as if you have been ruminating throughout your meditation, you are still gaining the benefits.

Meditators have also found, if they add the One Breath into their day consistently, their regular practice becomes easier to get into. They report that when they use the One Breath up to once per hour, their whole day becomes calmer.

If you are just starting, then it's best to begin with the breathing meditation. Gain some benefit from it before delving into other types of meditation. Once you have experience with it, this will help you get more from any other meditation you try.

In this meditation, you are using:

- Intentional Awareness (IA) to *know what's happening* with the breath.

- Restful Absorption (RA) to *calm the mind*.

- Engrossed Attention (EA) to *focus on the details and stay* with the breath.

- Question or Introspect (QI) (intuitively, along with periphery awareness) to *notice when your mind is wandering or distracted*.

- Authentic Attitudes (AA), namely, the beginner's mind. Be curious and interested in those sensations for anything new you may learn about them.

The breath, or sensations associated with the breath, may be moving, but you are still. Within EA, your observation point is still, even though the thing(s) you are observing may move.

Counting Breaths

You do not have to stop at one breath. The counting helps keep your mind focused. This focus helps to keep your mind steady long enough for you to become engrossed. How do you do it? Count silently, each in- and out-breath (breath in = one, breath out = two, breath in = three, etc.), up to ten.

Once you can count your breaths easily in this way, start counting only the in-breath (or out, but not both). Count them up to ten, then restart from one. If you can, do three rounds of ten without being distracted.

Your mind *wandering* is OK. This is where you are slightly distracted, but you can keep your attention also in your breath. After three rounds of ten, you may be able to let go of the counting completely. Whether you are ready will be assessed by how engrossed you feel.

How will I know I am 'engrossed'?

Remember, EA invites Restful Absorption (RA), so you will feel the effects of absorption:

- A numbness, or tingly, fuzzy sensation, which may feel pleasant.

- Your extremities disappear from your awareness.

- The outside world, and all those distractions, are no longer distracting. Your mind may still wander.

The above are part of the *cocoon effect* of RA. In addition, EA brings its own effects:

- You get drawn in, so the object will appear larger or closer.

- You notice more details about it (as you would if you put it under a microscope).

- It takes less effort to stay with your chosen object of meditation.

- Later, your awareness seems to stick to the object. It is harder to stop being in contact with it. Your mind wanders, but you don't get fully distracted.

The effects of being engrossed can be subtle. You may have to look for them to notice these signs.

Using a Word/Phrase Instead of Counting

You can also choose to say a word or phrase silently. Such as "In" for the in-breath and "Out" for the out-breath. The words (you say in your head) keep you focused on what you are aware of instead of numbers. You can also use other words, such as "Happy" or "Peace" or "Let go" or "Yes", etc. For example:

- If you feel OK with these words. In-breath, "Love", out-breath, "Peace"; in-breath, "Love", out-breath, "Peace".

- If you are working on relaxing more or letting go of stress. In-breath, "Release", out-breath, "Let go"; in-breath, "Release", out-breath, "Let go".

- If you want to encourage or motivate yourself. In-breath, "Yes", out-breath, "Yes"; in-breath, "Yes", out-breath, "Yes".

Tummy, Nostrils, or Whole-Body Breath?

You can expand upon the breathing meditation in various ways. Each has its benefits. Your focus changes depending on the stage you have reached in your practice.

If you are a beginner, the tummy is probably going to be easiest to focus on. But for some people, the easiest is the whole body (torso), and for a few others, it is the sensations in the nostrils.

There are nine stages to mastering Engrossed Attention (EA). To learn the subtleties of mastering EA, it's best to take part in a retreat guided by an expert. If you are interested in mastering EA, once you've developed a steady focus on the tummy, you will want to explore the smaller object (the nostrils).

In the later stages of mastering EA, you let go of the breath.

What About Focusing on a Candle?

Occasionally, someone tells me they have been using a candle for their meditation. This is a technique a lot of people have heard about. At first, it works to get you focused and it can induce the cocoon effect. Wonderful.

Some people do not realise that watching a candle is only the first part of the technique. You are supposed to shut (or half-close) your eyes as soon as you can remember what it looks like and visualise the candle. This brings in the mind-technology of Visualisation or Imagination (VI), so have a look at what I say in that chapter.

My recommendation is to not use a candle. Dr Allan Wallace tells us that in his 30+ years of study and practice of EA to mastery, it is best to use the breath as a focal point instead. Why? Western cultures put too much effort into their meditations – especially visualisations. You are likely to create an energy imbalance.

This doesn't mean you should never visualise. We are talking specifically about using a visualisation to master EA. The outward candle is OK if you only want to relax and enjoy the first stages of EA. If that works for you, that's great. If you want to take it further, or you are experiencing headaches, I recommend switching to the breath.

EA and visualisations are not the only meditations where people try too hard. You have read why putting too much effort into your meditation will hinder your progress. Read on to find out why meditation seems so difficult and seems to take forever to gain the benefits.

10

Myth: Meditation Is Too Difficult

THINGS THAT MAY MAKE meditation seem difficult are our tendencies to:

- Try too hard (see the chapter on *Myth: Try Hard To Succeed*).

- A wish to get it right.

- We can be overly attached to getting results.

Combined with other myths about *what you're trying to do* (e.g., to empty your mind), this becomes an impossible task – which defies your *attempts to get results*! I'm sure you can recognise how stressful that must be. We shall also look at other reasons meditation may seem too difficult: "I get too distracted", and "It takes too much effort to gain the benefits".

Do you try too hard?

This is such a big issue, I explore it after the next form of meditation, Engrossed Attention (EA).

Have you a wish to get it right?

This is one reason we try too hard. We are trying to get our meditation right. Although meditation is not collapsing on the sofa, you need to relax. The Authentic Attitudes (AA) will help you find a better approach to your meditation.

The wish to do it properly is one of my motivators. If it's yours, then this book is perfect for you. At first, I didn't have the balance right. My wish to get it right puts pressure on my meditations. I wasn't relaxing as much as is required to get it right.

We are all different. If you want to get it right, my instructions here should help. However, if you're still having problems, then contact me via the app. The problem can arise from not knowing which mind-technology to engage at specific moments in your meditation.

Restful Absorption(RA) is at the core of meditation for the whole of your meditations. Therefore, allowing rest is never a fault. Add a bit of Intentional Awareness and/or Engrossed Attention (EA) and you're definitely meditating.

Are you overly attached to getting results?

A psychology department at Newcastle University had me in for an experiment. The trainee scientists put one hundred electrodes on my scalp through a plastic cap. They checked on their computer to make sure they were all connected. Squiggly lines were being drawn in real-time on the graph shown on the screen.

They asked me to shut my eyes, but not to meditate. Almost immediately, I was told to open them and look at the screen. The chaotic lines had all plummeted to a smooth, straight line at the bottom of the chart. I was told, "This is the sign of a regular meditator." I realised it was showing a peaceful mind – result! Yes?

Yes, but only after I'd dropped any notion of trying to get *results* from meditation a decade before. Only after I'd worked out that I could get results – only if I carried out the *process* called meditation. I gave you the scoop on how meditation is a *process* in the chapter, *Myth: Try Hard To Succeed*.

There are many wonderful results of meditation, but trying to achieve them creates stress. Trying to get to the next stage in your practice can create too much stress for you to get there.

I Get Too Distracted

Meditation can help you have moments of stillness and peace. But when most people sit to meditate, they think they have developed Attention Deficit Hyperactivity Disorder (ADHD). Their mind distracts them. Their body distracts them. Emotions distract them.

In a world where businesses and others compete for your attention, it is hard to focus. Especially when you feel the overwhelm induced by the barrage of messages and drama. It's as if you have internalised the outside disharmony.

Under these conditions, it would seem almost impossible to meditate. Yet, if you run the process called meditation, your capsule will develop – despite the distractions. You will release bubbles of stress, despite the distractions. See the section within the chapter on Restful Absorption (RA) about *Release Bubbles Of Stress*.

Distractions are an expected part of your practice. Engrossed Attention (EA) has three parts:

1. You direct your awareness toward your chosen object of meditation.

2. You notice you're no longer attending to your object – you're distracted.

3. Gently, you bring your awareness back to the object, relax, and observe with interest, but without pushing, pulling, or controlling.

Notice number 2. Distractions are built into the system.

You are training your mind like you train a dog to "stay". Every time it moves, you gently place it back on its mat. Eventually, it recognises the command and what you want of it. People don't realise how untrained their mind is.

If you wouldn't give up on your dog's ability to learn, why give up on your mind? But please do not train your mind like a bully.

It Takes Too Long to Gain the Benefits

Some people believe it must take years of perseverance to receive any benefits from meditation. Thankfully, the benefits can be immediate as well as long-term.

For a few years, I was working for a charity as their Mindfulness Teacher. My job was to support a group of people with anxiety. While working with that group, I provided evidence of how a fifteen-minute meditation can reduce stress. I would ask them for their current stress-level, from one to ten. One would be completely chilled with zero stress. Ten may mean you feel panic.

At the start of our sessions, the group average was six to eight (highly stressed). After the meditation, the average came down by at *least* 50 per cent. Their stress dropped to an average of two to four (two = calm and relaxed).

Some new meditators say their sleep patterns have improved after just a few days of meditation practice. Scientific studies show a profound effect on people's physiology within weeks of starting a regular practice.

Every type of meditation described within these pages has many short- and long-term benefits. However, it's easy to dismiss those benefits because the mind forgets the issues you were dealing with.

How can you forget you had a problem?

Those problems are no longer important. In psychology, it is called the Apex Hypotheses. The hypothesis relates to when there is a shift in your circumstances that doesn't have a direct, logical cause. At the apex of your understanding, your *thinking* mind cannot understand the shift. The thinking mind cannot accept what happened (without an opening to greater intuition), so it will:

- Make something up to explain the shift, while ignoring any evidence to oppose the assumed cause.

- Decide the problem was never as big as you thought (instantly forgettable).

Meditators with a regular practice over years don't need the Apex Hypothesis to tell them about this phenomenon. In hindsight, they notice they no longer react to situations like they used to. At first, the changes can be subtle, and you may not have grown enough to recognise what's happening.

There is a mind-technology I've mentioned many times, which greatly enhances the therapeutic value of any meditation. It also helps you to grow in your practice quicker. It is a natural, authentic part of you that you will want to develop.

Before you discover how to apply the Authentic Attitudes (AA), let's look at what *attitudes* are. Plus, what might be getting in the way of them being the natural, sunny disposition of a regular meditator – and why that's not your fault.

11

Attitude

Your Attitudes Create Your Life

One's reaction – towards things, people, and oneself – is what we usually call an attitude.

Attitudes, in general psychology, are underlying trends, or patterns of thought, that have a feeling, or emotional element and lead you down a particular path of thinking or behaviour.

Psychologists define an attitude as:

> A learnt tendency to evaluate and react to things in a certain way.

This learnt tendency includes opinions about yourself, objects, people, issues, and events (anything).

How is it learnt?

1. You have an experience. Or you see or hear of what happened to someone else. Or you may experience or hear someone express their attitude.

2. There is a judgement of (you evaluate) the situation (e.g., thinking "it is good" or "it is bad").

3. You feel a certain way toward the thing or situation. Mostly based on your opinion of it.

4. You decide (not consciously) on your reaction to it. This updates your behaviour.

5. Other events will support your new attitude (maybe people agree it is good or bad, or you have repeating positive or negative experiences).

6. There is a change in your attitude over time because of new events or learning. The changes may mean the attitude becomes quieter or louder, but often it becomes more complex. The opinion (2 and 3 above) becomes a *belief*.

Your attitudes are based upon *beliefs* you hold, because of *opinions* you learned to have, a long time ago. A lot of this happens in childhood.

Examples

Frank has an attitude of not liking himself because:

1. Due to all the bad things he thinks he has done in his life (e.g., he was told picking his nose is bad, and all the other things adults tell kids to shame them into being good, so he concludes he is bad), Frank's present *experience* is that:

2. He *feels* shame but probably not consciously – maybe feeling empty instead.

3. He *believes* he is not good enough to be lovable (*evaluation/opinion*).

4. He withdraws from situations (*behaviour*) where someone may ask him to reveal his inner world.

Others may have a different reason for believing they are not good enough or are unlovable (this is their *belief* based upon what they have learnt because of their experience).

For instance:

1. Louise had a relationship with a bully who undermined her at all times (*experience*).

2. This has had an impact on her self-esteem and confidence, so she thinks she is (*evaluates* herself as) worthless (what she *learnt* from her experience – even though not true).

3. She *feels* fragile around other people, and the *thought* of being weak makes her *feel* anxious.

4. So she behaves (*reacts*) in ways to protect her fragile self-worth.

What they are *learning* (which turns into a *belief*) about themselves, along with the *feeling* and *behaviour*, are all part of the *reaction* they have. This creates their attitudes.

What people *learn* from their experience isn't always the truth. Often, the *evaluation* (opinion) is not the truth. Unfortunately, that opinion turns into a belief.

When reading the paragraph above, some may identify and feel tightness in their body. It may be in their chest or stomach, but it could be elsewhere. They might feel sad, or angry, or depressed, and empty of emotion and defeated.

Understandably, for such a person, the thought of being kind toward oneself is appealing. Yet, they also feel an overwhelming sense of doom and frustration about the possibility of being able to make it a consistent part of their life. They will immediately ask, "But how do I do it?"

You start from where you are, and take one step at a time. The meditation in Question or Introspect (QI) is a good place to begin untangling yourself from old beliefs and attitudes.

Emphasising the Authentic Attitudes (AA) in your meditations will help you on your path to wellness.

Before we explore the AA in the next chapter, I'd like you to know what happens when stress cuts you off from your *authentic* attitudes. It's important to know, so you can correct it. Meditation is supremely efficient at making the changes.

Distorted Side of Life

A lifetime of accumulated stress causes the imbalance that creates distortions in your thinking, attitudes, and emotions. There is a section on the app all about stress.

There are five main distorted (weather) patterns of attitude:

1. Whistling Winds of Cynicism

2. Foggy

3. Weeping Clouds of Emotional

4. Stormy

5. Whirlwind

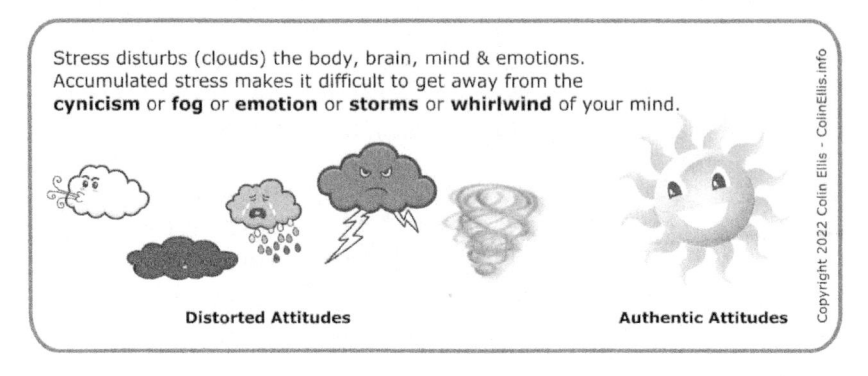

Stress disturbs (clouds) the body, brain, mind & emotions. Accumulated stress makes it difficult to get away from the **cynicism** or **fog** or **emotion** or **storms** or **whirlwind** of your mind.

Distorted Attitudes   Authentic Attitudes

The Authentic Attitudes (AA) are on the *natural* side of the map. It may be useful to explain what I mean by the five patterns on the *distorted* side. Accumulated stress causes a chemical imbalance in your body and brain, which creates the (weather) conditions of...

Whirlwind/Typhoon/Cyclone/Tornado

Because of the chemical imbalance, your brain is stuck on overdrive, pedalling like fury. But it doesn't know why, or how to get off the cycle-machine that's set at a high speed. You may think you have a hyperactive mind. Some common symptoms:

- A never-ending stream of thoughts.

- You cannot calm your mind.

- Projecting into the future with strategising, evaluating, assessing, creating, narrating, rehearsing, imagining, or worrying, etc.

- Ruminating on the past, by remembering, re-hashing dramas, establishing meaning, blaming, etc.

The thoughts are not always negative, but they are incessant. They may seem to go round and round – like being taken by a tornado, typhoon, or cyclone. I haven't even mentioned the whirlwind of emotions and thoughts that can come from desire. It could be natural, but if obsessive, there is a distortion due to stress.

Stormy/Thunderstorm

The weather changes fast sometimes, and you get caught in a thunderstorm. Your mind is angry, and it's as if you do not want to let go of the blame game. Such as:

- A minor storm of frustration, annoyance, irritability, impatience, or exasperation may catch you.

- Long-lasting dark clouds of displeasure, dissatisfaction, simmering resentment, bitterness, or agitation may follow you.

- Sometimes, it may be a full-blown thunder and lightning strike of anger, outrage, wrath, or temper tantrum.

Although these sound negative, they are the symptoms of long-term stress effecting your brain and distorting your mind.

Weeping Clouds: of Feeling Emotional/Sensitive/Distressed/Anxious

A cloud bursting into tears produces a warm downpour, letting go of its burden. If you hear yourself described as 'too sensitive', your system is reacting to an overload of stress. I use the word *stress* in a very broad sense, so it also includes trauma and all kinds of loss. Maybe you:

- Cry for no reason.
- Feel sad, upset, anxious or depressed.
- Have positive emotions or desires that feel too intense.

Indio-Tibetan medical scholars say these symptoms show an energy imbalance. Whether it is an energy imbalance or a chemical imbalance, the cause is the same – accumulated stress affecting your emotional systems.

Fog

When a cloud drops to earth, or the mist rises, you can find yourself lost in fog. In the same way, your brain can get foggy:

- With a blank screen of confusion.
- You can feel disoriented, as the bright sparks of creativity seem to have dissipated.
- In this state, you can easily attain the blank slate of an empty mind.
- Distractions are not a problem while in the fog. It feels good to be good at something.

It can feel as if you have a gift for meditation. You could believe you can easily get into the cocoon I described in the chapter on Restful Absorption (RA). Without a clear head to compare your experience, the lifeless fog may obscure grogginess. Yet, this is another way in which stress can cause disruption in your brain, which dulls your ability to think clearly.

Whistling Wind of Cynicism

The others – an angry storm, a weepy cloud of emotion, the confusion of a foggy mind – are easier to recognise.

The whistling wind of a scoffing, incredulous, sceptical mind is harder to accept within oneself.

- Pessimism is seen as being realistic.
- Pedantic is honouring your language and wanting clarity.
- We need to be sceptical, or we will be fooled.
- The same for being suspicious, distrusting, and jaundiced by life.

I chose the whistling wind to symbolise this cynical approach because the wind is indifferent to most things. It can make it extremely hard to believe meditation can help. You may *want* to believe. You can find scientific evidence to support the fact meditation is beneficial. Yet that doesn't stop the mind from doing its best to sabotage your efforts. Not because some part of you wants to be this way, but because of the imbalance of stress chemicals the brain is dealing with.

One way the brain tries to deal with stress is to hold rigidly to the left brain tasks that are made for survival. Your thoughts become fear-based: seeing the separation clearly and focused on the past or material knowledge. It is a form of disassociation.

You're cut off from the right brain, which would normally make you open to connection, empathy, and the wonder of life. Yes, there are a lot of excellent parts of the left brain, such as logic. But you also need the right brain.

You do not want the negative side of being in a stale, mechanistic world of the left brain to dominate. Not simply because stress has cut you off from the wholeness of who you are.

Why It's Not Your Fault

In the book *Stress, Anxiety and the Battle for Your Sanity*, I tell you:

- How your attitudes depend on your brain chemistry.

- Your brain chemistry depends on the hormones and other chemicals created by your body.

- The chemistry in your body depends on the amount of stress stockpiled in your life and your ability to release it.

I mentioned the problem of the stress barrel. In childhood, your ability to process stress is like an open cylinder. Over time, it's as if the cylinder is becoming calcified due to stress. With enough stress, the cylinder becomes more like a barrel with a tiny hole.

Once full, your barrel has no more capacity. Even a small amount of stress creates feelings of being overburdened. The body is no longer releasing the chemicals created by stressful situations, so more of it goes (and stays) in the brain, affecting your mind.

When stress chemicals affect your mind, it can no longer function at an optimum level. It is squeezed into fear-based, left brain thinking.

Stress (in all its forms) causes distorted minds, emotions, and many physical ailments. It's not your fault:

- Life in the 21st century is stress-chemical inducing.

- Your body reactions create the chemicals associated with stress. It's a good thing – to save you from danger.

- After decades of processing stress, your body now has less capacity to deal with it.

- The chemicals accumulate over time.

- The accumulated chemicals can flood the brain, and with no method for release, will sit there.

- It's not your fault the accumulated stress chemicals in your brain can have a toxic influence on your mind, attitude, and emotions.

Thankfully, there are pioneering methods (without drugs of any kind) that can help reduce the overload. To get myself out of chronic stress and anxiety, I used a combination of methods. Meditation is the one I kept coming back to because of its ability to release stress. Although the app is new, I suspect the section on stress will become a big part of the help provided.

We have covered what an attitude is, and how your Authentic Attitudes (AA) can be clouded over (distorted) by stress. Now it's time to turn our attention to the Authentic Attitudes (AA) and how to let them shine.

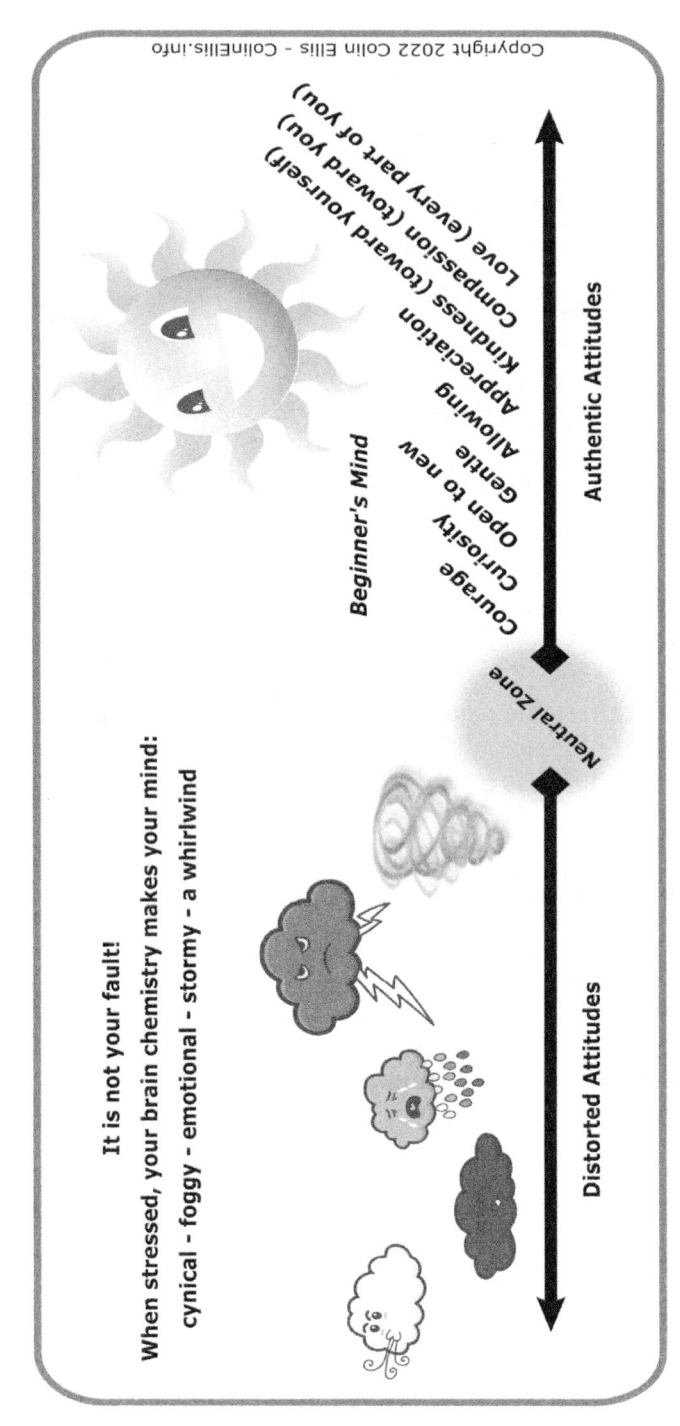

Meditation gets you to the Neutral Zone, then helps you *nudge* along the Authentic Attitudes

Authentic Attitudes

Love (every part of you)
Compassion (toward you)
Kindness (toward yourself)
Appreciation
Allowing
Gentle
Open to new
Curiosity
Courage

Beginner's Mind

Neutral Zone

Distorted Attitudes

It is not your fault!

When stressed, your brain chemistry makes your mind:
cynical - foggy - emotional - stormy - a whirlwind

Copyright 2022 Colin Ellis - ColinEllis.info

12

Authentic Attitudes (AA)

IF YOU WANT TO fly through the Universe, you need a spacecraft.

An IntrAnaut also needs a space vehicle. Restful Absorption (RA) creates the perfect space capsule. You want to make sure you have a meditation capsule (RA) where you can sit (IA) comfortably and safely.

You will decide on which direction you want to travel. Engrossed Attention (EA) points you toward what you want to know. Plus, your capsule needs to be self-contained, so nothing of value drifts off into space. EA keeps you inside your meditation.

Brilliant! You have your spacecraft. It is safe, comfortable, and secure, and you can direct it to where you want to go. But what's missing?

Fuel.

As this is an analogy for your meditation capsule into your inner space, what is the fuel? The missing piece comes from the Authentic Attitudes (AA). They are not a core part of every meditation, but maybe they should be.

You will find your AAs are completely natural and can arise from every human without the need to create them. However, most people have come away from their natural essence so much that instead of the natural AAs, we experience distorted minds.

We are in the ludicrous position of teaching people how to experience their natural qualities. The AAs nudge you toward expressing your natural calm, joy, and kindness. The ultimate fuel for meditation is the unforced side-effect of the AAs I shall describe in this chapter.

One way to illustrate the Authentic Attitudes (AA) is to use the analogy of the sky. At one end of the diagram is a clear, blue sky, without a cloud to be seen, and the sun shining brightly.

At the other end, the sky is full of clouds. The clouds obscure the sun and sky. It can get dark on that side. Possibly, with rain, fog, or storms of thunder and lightning. This cloudy weather *obscures or distorts the light*. The sunny half is *clear* (of clouds/distortions) and *natural*.

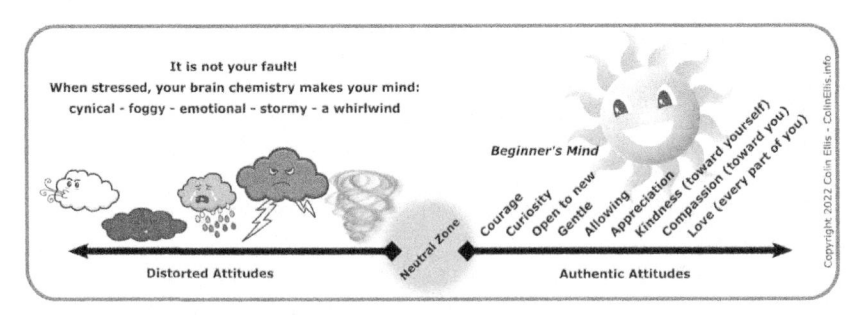

It is not your fault!
When stressed, your brain chemistry makes your mind: cynical - foggy - emotional - stormy - a whirlwind

Beginner's Mind

Courage, Curiosity, Open to new, Gentle, Allowing, Appreciation (toward yourself), Kindness (toward you), Compassion (every part of you), Love

Distorted Attitudes — Neutral Zone — Authentic Attitudes

Copyright 2022 Colin Ellis - ColinEllis.info

Meditation gets you to the Neutral Zone, then helps you to nudge along the Authentic Attitudes (AA).

Neutral Zone

The first the AA is the neutral zone. Here, you are without positive or negative opinions. Most mindfulness teachers call this space 'non-judgemental'.

What regular meditators notice within the neutral zone is peace. This peace is what you feel when your mind is *clear of the clouds of distorted thinking*. Sometimes, the neutral zone is described as *a feeling of contentment*.

Synonyms for peace are – depending on the facet you perceive – calm, stillness, space, blank, empty, void, nothingness, and serenity.

From here, you can nudge yourself along the Authentic Attitudes (AA).

Do you feel no peace when sitting down to meditate?

The first few AA can help you get there. Restful Absorption (RA), and Engrossed Attention (EA), are excellent for uncovering your natural calmness.

How is peace felt in the neutral zone different from a foggy mind?

If you have a foggy mind, it is hard to know the difference. One sign of a foggy mind is when you can drop into a blank space easily. You are without distraction or a chatty mind. But this is before you have developed a regular practice.

You may feel more numb than alive and conscious. Your practice does not lead to more clarity, and the contentment doesn't give way to a pleasant feeling or joy.

Only when you have a meditation that is lucid, joyful, and free of subtle slumber will you be able to observe the difference. Although your practice may not yet be there, you now have a clearer idea of what to look for. You can make adjustments and use the AA to help.

How do you get to the neutral zone?

Restful Absorption (RA) and Engrossed Attention (EA) are the easiest vehicles to get you to the neutral zone. Others can do it, but you'll find it is because RA and EA are engaged (consciously or implied). If you are using a mantra, for instance, the rhythm will help to activate RA, and focusing on the verbal syllables will engage EA.

Be Gentle on Yourself

No matter what happens, be gentle on yourself.

To be gentle on yourself is (in my opinion) the most important of the Authentic Attitudes (AA).

Being gentle on yourself is more than words. It is an attitude you can feel. It is a gateway to healthier meditation, and links into the other Authentic Attitudes (AA). Being gentle opens the door to healing and insights. Without it, you can get trapped in a quagmire of distorted minds. Once this happens, you can easily find yourself feeling anxious, fearful, or depressed.

How do you do being gentle?

Think for a moment about how you'd support a friend in a crisis. You may say soothing words of encouragement that acknowledge how they feel.

People get upset towards their own pain, negativeness, and worries, adding more stress to the situation. This reminds me of the two arrows.

What are the two arrows?

The monk gave his teaching as I sat looking up, cross-legged, on the hard floor. I listened, while complaining internally about the pain in my ankle. "I should have gotten an extra cushion. I'm so stupid! Why does this always happen to me? Well, I'm now fully attentive and awake – to this pain!"

While I focused on the misfortune of having boney ankles, the monk told us about the two arrows. The *first arrow* is the pain you will suffer because of being alive in a human body. That is pain (physical, mental, or emotional), loss, trauma (big and small), and stress of all kinds.

The *second arrow* is optional and shot by yourself. We shoot this arrow when we blame ourselves or others for our misfortune. It is when we give our pain/stress greater meaning than the fact that life in a body is stressful/painful. The apparent cause doesn't matter because illness, ageing, and death are inevitable.

What matters is whether you deserve the second arrow that only you can inflict. Any thoughts that do <u>not</u> go toward relieving your pain are probably a second, third, or fourth arrow!

There is a way to be supportive (an alternative to, *trying to be positive)*. When my friend is feeling bad, one thing I do to support them is to have an attitude and energetic environment where rest, or time-out, is available.

You can do the same for you! No need for any words. Decide to relax. Relax about the situation for a moment. Relax away from the negative thinking for a moment, and relax in a gentle, supportive manner. You can see how meditation can help with this.

Relax into It

Another term for being gentle is to relax. Being gentle, to a large extent, is about relaxing your rigid views. Relax your determination to be right, revenged, secure, in control, achieve, or to win the internal battle. It is a decision to have a rest. Being gentle on yourself means to stop trying to control your thoughts and feelings. It means to allow yourself to feel crap, exhausted, resistant, angry, frustrated or however you are feeling right now. Decide to relax and be gentle with yourself.

Being gentle can start with a decision to relax (which is more accessible than determining how you must think). Then choose to be gentle (as if with a friend in need). This immediately starts creating a better environment in your brain and body. Relaxing into being gentle also helps you into the neutral zone.

Continue to produce an internal eco-system for your mind and body to flourish:

- Acknowledge it is not your fault and your mind cannot help – but meditation can.

- Meditate to release accumulated stress from the past.

- Work on the Authentic Attitudes (AA). Such as being gentle, appreciation, allowing, etc. By doing so, you install a positive internal environment (without having to think positive thoughts).

- Know how to pull it all together and gain additional support (maybe via the app).

If you find you cannot fully relax and be gentle, see if the *beginner's mind* (below) can serve you better. Even if you can be gentle, the beginner's mind will help you develop your meditation practice in significant ways.

Beginner's Mind

When teaching meditation, I often relate to the meditation we're about to do, as *an experiment*. I'm using the method: do an experiment and observe exactly what you're experiencing. This is part of the beginner's mind. There is a section on *Goals vs Experiment* in the chapter, *Myth: You Never Fall Back*, where I answer the question *"How do you approach an experiment?"*

If you want to get the most from your meditation practice, my advice is to come to it with a beginner's mind. When adults come across something for the first time, they can be cautious. Adults will constantly compare whatever they come across with past events and preferences. A child, however, may be curious and open to learning from this new experience. With no preconceptions. The mind of the child is a beginner's mind.

> A beginner has a mind that doesn't have the answer. They are open to their expectations being incorrect. They are open to new insights.

The beginner's mind comes out of the neutral zone and employs some characteristics from that zone:

- Not getting involved with expectations.

- Not getting involved with evaluating, comparing, or analysing.

- Not getting involved with judging, guessing, or preferences.

"Not getting involved with" means the mind is *doing what it does,* but you have decided your object of meditation is more interesting. These types of thinking appear, but you ignore them.

By exercising your Authentic Attitudes (AA), your mind will quieten as you ignore its prompts. With training in a beginner's mind, you will be able to watch the mind *do its thing.*

Mind and Body – *Doing Its Thing*

While you engage in the body scan, you may notice the various sensations appear without deliberately creating them. During that meditation, you are observing your body *do its thing*. You may recognise you have little control over what's happening – other than to look away.

When you have enough training to observe your physical sensations, you are ready to watch your mind. With the understanding that your body *does its thing*, you may quickly notice your mind is the same.

When I am observing my mind, I often find I am listening to a narration of what I'm reading or doing. At other times, the voice is rehearsing future conversations or re-hashing old ones. Just as your body breathes: comparison, evaluation, and analysing are what the mind does.

Let's look at the components of a beginner's mind. There are three. With the beginner's mind, you add:

- **Curiosity**. You are paying attention, with interest.

- **Openness** – to anything new that you can learn from the experience.

- **Courage** – to let go of the old and welcome the new. It's daunting to face your mind, or the outside world, with an open mind.

This list is ideal, and at first, will not happen quickly for most adults. An adult's mind will automatically judge, evaluate, and have preconceived ideas about what it is they perceive.

How to Begin Using the Beginner's Mind

Attempt to be non-judgemental, or *neutral*, in your attitude toward your frailties. Attempt to be *gentle* with yourself on your new journey.

As well as dropping your involvement in thoughts – as best you can at the moment – you are interested in your chosen object. Your intentions and questions for your meditation will help you be *curious*. Your interest in your object will help you be *open* to learning more about it.

Attempt to accept that whatever attitudes, thoughts, behaviours, etc., you have now, are simply the place where you are starting from.

Allowing

In mindfulness circles, there is a lot of emphasis on acceptance. Here is the brief definition:

At this moment, y*ou are **allowing** your reality to exist.*

Let's first look at what this Authentic Attitude (AA) is <u>not</u> asking us to accept.

We do not ask you to allow:

- Any negative judgments and physical feelings you have <u>*means*</u> you are bad, useless, worthless, or broken, etc.

- Any negative minds and physical sensations you have are now an *intrinsic* part of your life from now on.

- The negative thoughts and physical reactions *are who you are*.

- The negative thoughts and physical phenomena are *chosen by you* or wanted.

What are you allowing?

> Allow the present moment, and everything in it, to be as it is: full stop.

The present moment has already come into existence. Once you have noticed it, it is already in the past. You cannot change it! Accept it already exists, and you cannot change it. Resistance is futile!

It reminds me of the King Canute story, proving even a king cannot stop the sea tide. It is said King Canute tried to prove his royalty was god-like. He stood on the shoreline, commanding the sea to stop the tide coming in.

They used the story as an analogy. The non-acceptance of the tide of time is a recipe for frustration and an act of futility. You can imagine any such consistent act of futility will have a detrimental effect on a person's self-esteem.

Allowing means allowing that right now, at this moment, "My mind is *doing its thing*, and my body is being how it is."

At first, this is hard to do – which is why the AAs are a process.

Through meditation, you will gain an insight into the fact your mind is not who you are. You can be clear it is not you, thereby gaining the strength to do this outside of meditation.

Initially, your distorted instincts may be too strong and jump all over your attempts to be *allowing* of anything. Being *gentle* toward yourself will help, as will the training in *appreciation*.

Appreciation

Lots of people think that it's impossible to fall in love with life. And yet others do exactly that. How can that be?

Intentional Awareness (IA) is about where you put your attention. Where your intention is, is where your awareness is. If you intend to see beauty, that's where your attention goes, and what your awareness perceives.

Appreciation can help with changing your awareness, from ugly to beauty.

What is appreciation, and how can you use it?

The word *appreciation* is being used in a specific way.

> Appreciation of something is the recognition and enjoyment of its good qualities. ~ Collins Dictionary [1]

---

1. Collins Dictionary, 06/2022, https://www.collinsdictionary.com/dictionary/english/appreciation

In the context of your meditation practice, appreciation is about what you can see, hear, smell, taste, touch, or perceive in your mind. You are looking for something within your environment (external or internal) to appreciate. By that, I mean you can say "That's OK."

Appreciation is mostly an *informal* practice. However, the more you use it outside meditation, the more pleasant your meditations will become.

Initially, I ask students to find something about which their reaction is only slightly above indifference. Apply this method with patience and you will notice your reaction changing. Start with at least a "Hmm, that's OK". You may react to some things with a "Wow!", but that's not what it needs to be. An "Ah, that's OK", is OK.

What if I cannot find anything that has any good qualities?

When I got a new camera, I was excited. I wanted to see how it would handle zooming in to photograph the fine details of a flower. A macro button on the camera solved the problem. It could automatically zoom in and adjust the lens so I'd take a perfect, close-up photo.

I advise students to "Go macro." By which, I mean they should look for something small, possibly tiny. It only has to take a moment. Here are some examples:

- The slither of light shining from behind the curtain. The twinkle on the edge of a glass.
- The shape of a shadow across the couch. The colour of the logo on a can.
- The warmth of your body.
- The feel or texture of your clothes.
- A sound, or lack of sound, between the noises.
- The after-taste of your meal.

You have five senses to explore and look for anything in your environment to appreciate. Just for a moment, or for longer if available. If you truly cannot find anything within your external environment, then seek something inside. Imagine being in nature and *appreciate* what appears, or what it feels like.

Do this at least twelve times every day when you remember.

Immediately, when you remember you haven't done this for a while; be gentle on yourself and look around for something to appreciate. If you don't find something, go macro. When you find something, congratulate yourself, as a reminder to your deeper mind this is something you want more of.

Don't forget to use appreciation within your meditations. Your meditations will improve quicker and the benefits in your life will appear faster.

Isn't this gratitude?

Some people use the words *gratitude* and *appreciation* as synonyms. I do that sometimes. Gratitude is being thankful for the things you have already received. You can also be thankful for what you experience in the present moment.

In this practice, within the Authentic Attitudes (AA), the word *appreciation* is a better fit. Appreciation is about what is observable to you right now. You may not have been aware of it a few moments ago. Like a rainbow, it could be gone in the next moment.

Without appreciation, gratitude is unreasonable to muster.

Kindness

Kindness toward yourself, to a certain extent, is simply to not judge yourself. Refrain from beating yourself up about whatever thoughts or feelings you have right now. That's why, in the diagram of Authentic Attitudes (AA), kindness appears after gentleness, allowing, and appreciation.

> You are being kind to yourself by gently allowing yourself to experience beauty – no matter how small.

Be Kind! *But how do you do that?*

Nudge along the Authentic Attitudes (AA):

1. The neutral zone of not being positive or negative.

2. The courage to be open and curious.

3. Allowing everything that already exists so you don't fall into the trap of futility.

4. Deliberately seek to appreciate the beauty in your environment – including in people and in yourself.

5. You will automatically *be kind* – without trying.

You don't need to create a feeling of kindness. Kindness arises spontaneously at this stage on the Authentic Attitudes (AA).

Trust is an element of kindness – for it is hard to feel kind toward something we do not trust. Trusting your thoughts, instinct or intuition can be extremely hard. Especially when another part of you knows those thoughts are not accurate or useful.

Most people have a skewed idea of what their mind is and what it is supposed to do. They believe their mind is *who they are.* Therefore, if there is faulty thinking, then they themselves are faulty. "How could you trust something that's so faulty? You wouldn't trust the reading on a faulty meter!" This, however, is faulty thinking.

I've mentioned how the body and mind *do their own thing*. If the mind was truly you, your intention would be enough to direct your thoughts, or silence them. The fact your mind doesn't obey your intention is proof the thoughts are not you.

Your thoughts and body are parts of your experience. An important part, because of your identification with them. Ultimately, they are not you, even though you carry them with you all the time.

You could say they are the crucial parts of what you have to work with in your life. You are living through them, but they are not who you are.

That sounds philosophical. Meditation is not a philosophy: it is a tool. By using meditation in your daily life, you can gain a clear insight into this truth. Not immediately, but slowly, over time. To know from direct experience (not philosophy) who and what you are is at the heart of awakening. The first step is to recognise – from direct experience – what you are not.

What has this got to do with kindness?

I'm setting the stage for being precise about what you are being kind toward. It is *you* who is being kind, and kindness is an authentic quality of who you are. Kindness is a *part of you.* The negative, judgemental, distorted parts are what you are being kind toward.

This slight distance – between you (who is *aware)*, and the thoughts or feelings you are kind toward – can help with allowing and kindness.

What about love and compassion?

You may hear meditation teachers talk about *Loving Kindness, Love,* or *Compassion*. I associate these terms with kindness.

Love has various elements: trust, appreciation, and joyful feelings. Notice, I also associate trust and appreciation with kindness.

Children, when they first learn about *love* say the word often: "I love this", "I love that", when you might say "I like this" or "I like that." The kids are expressing their appreciation and really feeling it. *Love* and *like* can be interchangeable. The only difference seems to be the amount of joyful feeling associated with the appreciation we have.

Loving Kindness is a halfway house between a feeling of kindness (appreciation) toward someone or something and the joy of love.

Compassion comes from feeling kindness (or love) toward a person, animal, bird, or fish and then seeing it upset or in pain. We can interpret it as *a wish for them to be out of pain*.

Kindness can also mean giving yourself encouragement. Kind words to give yourself a break from the judgement. To reassure yourself things will be OK, or will get better. No matter how horrible it is for you right now, it will not last forever, and shall change.

Meditation: Inner Smile

The *Authentic Attitudes* (AA) are what you want to emphasise in every meditation. They arise naturally and are therapeutic. You can *nudge* yourself along the continuum that makes up these attitudes – from having a neutral attitude (neither positive nor negative), to being gentle, the beginner's mind, and so on. A smile is a shortcut to kindness. This meditation brings your Authentic Attitudes (AA) to the foreground:

1. Settle into a comfortable position – sitting, standing, or lying – with eyes open or closed. Relax.

2. Scan your body for any tension. If you find any tension, gently release it, let it go, and allow all the muscles in that area to relax deeply and fully.

3. Use the beginner's mind with the One Breath meditation on the torso area (tummy and chest) until your mind becomes quieter. If your mind is not settling,

decide to relax and be gentle with yourself.

4. Think of something for which you feel thankful, or is funny. Feel yourself smile. Deliberately smile. Appreciate the feeling.

5. Focus on the smile, and take note of how it feels in your body (not just your face and head).

6. Use your imagination to let that feeling expand – away from your face. Appreciate the feeling and decide to have a kind attitude toward your body, mind, and any emotions that appear.

7. Let go of the facial expression, but allow it to be there if smiling is happening with no effort.

8. Focus on the feeling of your inner smile as it fills a bigger part of your awareness. Notice how that feels and appreciate it.

9. Slowly point your inner smile toward your feet, *then* legs, pelvis, abdomen, lower back, chest, upper back, shoulders, neck, and head. Use appreciation and thankfulness for each part of your body to reignite the inner smile.

10. Gently, slowly, bring yourself out of meditation. Bring the feelings with you, so they permeate your attitude toward your external world. Wiggle your toes and fingers, have a stretch, and be aware of your body and surroundings. If your eyes are shut, allow them to open gently in their own time. If it's bright, put your palms over your eyes for extra gentleness.

Nuggets

How you feel depends on how stressed you are. If depressed, you may only gain a neutral feeling from this meditation initially. If you have meditated a lot, it could induce bliss!

When stress is no longer distorting your mind and emotions, it is easier for your warm emotions to emerge. We could extend all the meditations within these pages. Extending this inner smile meditation has the potential to change your life!

You have FREE access to the full meditations on audio. Download the IntrAnaut mobile app, *Meditation & Wellbeing*, and use the code on the page at the end of the chapter, *Resources and What Next?*

For many, the desire to do (not rest) is the reason, *creating* with their imagination is so enticing. But do they have the wrong idea about Visualisations or Imagination (VI) style meditations?

13

Myth: I Cannot Visualise

AT THE MEDITATION CLASSES I attended in the '90s, they guided me in various visualisations. These seemed easier than trying to stop myself from getting involved with thoughts. I simply had to follow the guidance, then generate the visuals on command. I was rubbish at visualisation.

The images were so fleeting, and I was hardly conscious of their contents. It was tough, but I'd do my best to get it right. Unfortunately, my mind would dive into daydreams and distract me from the images I was supposed to be creating.

I thought, "I need more control." Without realising it, I was again creating the perfect conditions for more headaches, more frustration, and more distracting thoughts. Thankfully, I asked for help.

But I Cannot Visualise

There are two basic problems people find with visualisation:

1. They think the VISUALisation needs to be a Hi-Definition, full-colour movie they play in their head. This is the easiest and quickest way to make your meditation into a headache-inducing nightmare.

2. They believe it needs to be visual. Nope!

For most people, there are visual elements, but your Visualisation or Imagination (VI) can be on the creative side. It doesn't need to be visual at all. There are details below about how to do it without the visual element. And before you say, "I'm not imaginative", let's do an experiment.

- Remember the time when ..... [add one of your best memories here] ....

Does a memory pop up? It could be from five minutes ago, or years. What matters is you can tell me about it (no matter how vague).

It is your creative, intuitive mind that gives you the ability to do this. I know you may have been told creativity isn't about memory. For meditation, you do not need to have any more of a creative ability than the creation of memories.

Memories are not data dumps you can access, like a DVD. They are re-created each time you want to access them. Memories that are accessed most often are easier to recreate. Please feed your brain with all the good times.

Is there anything in your life you would like to do again? Maybe something that makes you feel amazing! Can you remember it?

1. Can you envision doing that again?

2. When you bring up that memory, does it bring up any feelings?

3. If not immediately, can you access the feelings you had – even if subdued – if you try. Don't push; relaxing helps.

4. When imagining doing it again, is there a vague flash of an image associated with the event?

5. When imagining doing it again, are there thoughts describing it?

6. When thinking of doing it again, do you just know the answer? Do you have a sense of what may happen?

If you said "Yes" to any of the above, you are using the technology of Visualisation or Imagination (VI). How? Read on for an answer. The six points below relate to the six just above.

1. If you can contemplate doing something in the future – even without visuals or it being different to your experiences in the past – you are using VI.

2. Some people have a greater connection to their ability to *feel*.

3. Your VI could be mostly recognisable by the *feelings* the non-*visualisation* creates in you.

4. For the vast majority who say they can visualise, the imagery is vague and fleeting. That is normal, and you should not try to make it clear.

5. For some people, their verbal thinking is dominant, which means they describe (or sometimes see words) instead of imagery or feelings. Your descriptive thoughts are your way of imagining.

6. You are using the intuitive faculty, which needs no words, feelings, or imagery. You have a sense of what is happening, and that is enough.

Everyone has all the mental abilities:

- Visual

- Audio (auditory)

- Feeling (kinesthetic)

- Intuitive knowing

For most people, one is primary. If your primary mental focus is other than a prowess for imagery, it may seem as if you cannot visualise. However, you can still imagine (VI) with your principal ability.

You can also work on allowing the other faculties to develop. Do this by noticing even the slightest glimmer and celebrating the tiniest of achievements.

Have you ever woken up from a dream because you heard a sound, then realised the sound must have been a part of your dream? Have you ever woken from a dream and remembered a part of it? Hearing sounds within a dream is proof you can create sounds in your mind. To remember having a dream is proof of your ability to imagine.

Fake It Till You Make It

There are too many wannabes faking it so they can make it in the world. Hype rules over substance. Yet, with your imagination, I fully recommend you go along with guided meditations as if you can connect with all aspects of the visualisation.

For instance, I found a particular meditation difficult. They instructed us to connect with a spark of light at the heart as a direct link to the infinite Self. I couldn't feel the connection (it just felt fake to me). But I could *imagine* a connection, despite it feeling fake, so I dispensed with disbelief.

When you *fake it* when allowing your intuitive mind to use the narrative for healing, then it can be a beneficial meditation. If you get hung up on the validity of the details, it will have no benefit.

On a basic level, by pretending you can meditate (while not deluding oneself that things that are not meditation actually are), you are facilitating your practice. For example, if focused on the breath at the nostrils, but unable to feel the sensations, you have choices. One of which is to pretend you can and see what happens.

The paradox is between: pretending to meditate, and knowing what is actual meditation. Yet they can be the same. I am pretty sure a lot of my meditations have been pretend, yet I have still progressed.

14

Visualisation or Imagination (VI)

VISUALISATION OR IMAGINATION (VI) style meditations are among the most prolific. People love visualisation, don't they? You can add a VI at the beginning; either before or after the relaxation. You can add a VI at the end. Or use VI throughout your meditation.

There are a few things I'd like to mention so you feel more comfortable with visualisations.

Blind Faith and Visualisation or Imagination (VI)

> "Dispensing With Dis-belief." That's my new mantra. Ha ha ha. ~ Q.C. Ellis

I remember when I first visited a Buddhist centre. When it was time to meditate, I became rigid in fear of being hypnotised into believing their philosophy. I'm not into having blind faith.

Eventually, I could relax because there was not much I didn't already believe. Where the imagery was obscure, they could explain the reasons for them to my satisfaction.

An issue with visualisations I come across is the person who is rational and, like me, doesn't want to engage in blind faith. This is how to approach visualisations if you too have this ideal.

When you watch a sci-fi movie, do you engage your rational mind and dismiss everything that isn't 'real'? Of course not. You suspend disbelief so you can be entertained.

It is the same with meditation. You suspend disbelief while meditating to give your intuitive mind the space to do its thing.

Ask any psychologist and they will tell you, your mind is extremely powerful. Your mind loves stories and can use them as metaphors to heal the past. You may have noticed how some stories can really touch your emotions.

When watching a movie, does suspending disbelief – and having an emotional reaction to the fake (sometimes bizarre) scenes – make you believe in anything that is not real? Never!

It is the same when you are meditating. By allowing your imagination to create narratives with imaginary scenes and beings, you are giving your intuitive mind the food (metaphors, analogies, and parables) it needs to heal the parts your conscious mind cannot reach. It is as if your deeper mind says, "YES! A chance to do healing work."

The intuitive part of your mind can use whatever imagery you give it to do that work. Your rational, conscious mind has nothing that can help in this process. Except get out of the way.

Visualisation or Imagination (VI) is not asking for blind faith. You are not opening yourself up to believing something your conscious mind would reject. By suspending disbelief during guided VI, you are allowing your mind to do its most profound work.

Is Every Visualisation a Meditation?

Shamans use Visualisation or Imagination (VI) when journeying. They may start by imagining standing at the foot of a tree. Visualising a hole between the roots, they imagine shrinking to journey down a tunnel into the underworld. Or instead, they may envisage becoming as light as a feather so they can clamber up the tree toward the upper realms.

These are not the only realms a shaman may explore. Nor is this the only way for them to nudge themselves into the journey. But you get the picture. Shamans say *your intention is like an arrow* pulling you into other realms. You relax as your mind travels into a dreamscape where communication with other beings can emerge.

The conversation on the reality (or not) of shamanic journeys is beyond this book. What matters is the message they receive is beneficial.

Journeying *is meditation* because you allow inspiration to surface once your intention and initial nudge are set in motion.

Hypnotherapy uses visualisation. There are two major forms of hypnosis: directed and non-directed.

Suggestions that command your mind characterise directed hypnosis. To use direct commands, you tell your mind what you want. To do this, you must know what the best result will be. Notice how this is about control.

Non-directed hypnotherapy makes suggestions your mind can employ or not. When a hypnotherapist uses non-directed suggestions, they allow the highest parts of the person's mind to decide what's best.

You want confidence? The guide will use metaphors to show *confidence* as a wholesome quality you possess. Encouraging your mind to choose and expand your natural qualities.

Directed hypnosis is <u>not</u> meditation. Non-directed hypnotherapy is meditation with specialist techniques.

A sports psychologist will advise players to visualise themselves going through a routine with perfect precision. Are they therefore meditating?

It depends. It is a mental activity. You are focusing your attention inward. You may intentionally know what you are doing in your imagination.

Are you relaxing? Are you moving toward, or further from, Restful Absorption (RA)?

Visualising in a way that's tight, controlling, or trying to make the visuals clearer is not meditation. However, if you bring *fun* into your visualisations, then you are probably meditating.

Daydreaming is not meditation without intentionally nudging your mind to explore.

Meditation: Sunny Beach to De-stress

If you see yourself as someone who is good at visualising, don't skip the previous chapter on the *Myth: I Cannot Visualise*. There are some useful gems for you too.

Here is one example of the countless meditations utilising your imagination:

1. Get yourself comfortable, either sitting or lying, and close your eyes.

2. Scan your body for any tension. If you feel any, release and let it go. Allow the muscles in that area to relax fully.

3. [Optional] Use the One Breath meditation until you feel a little calmer.

4. Allow yourself to imagine you are standing by a tropical beach. The sun is shining, and you can feel the warmth on your skin.

5. Step onto the sand, and walk along the beach, feeling the warmth beneath your feet.

6. Over there is a shallow pool under the shade of a palm tree. Once there, you dip a toe in, and realise

it is wonderfully warm; exactly the right temperature. You get into the pool, with your head cradled as if on a pillow and your body only just submerged. Feel the warm support under your body as you surrender to the embrace of the sand.

7. Feel any stress melt into the pool as you relax more deeply. Feel any worries wash away. The salty water draws out any negative energy from you. The warm water soothes you, softening the resistance to let go.

8. Allow yourself to let go of any tension. Let go of any stresses or strains. Let go of any tightness in your body or mind.

9. As you let go, imagine a cloud forms up there in the sky. The more you let go, the bigger the cloud becomes.

10. Let go of any beliefs that limit you. Let go of any blame, fears, or feeling like a victim. The cloud gets bigger.

11. And when you are ready, having let go of all that's right to let go of today, the cloud blows out to sea.

12. Out in the far distance, you can imagine the cloud letting go of its burden. And as is the way with nature, there appears a rainbow: a symbol of transformation. Nature transforms the distorted energies you released into life-affirming energies for others.

13. When you're ready, imagine you get up from the pool and dry off in the sun as you walk back to the edge of the beach. You can come back at any time: to release stress, let go of distorted energies or beliefs, and refreshen your body and soul.

14. Gently, slowly, bring yourself out of meditation. Wiggle your toes and fingers; maybe have a stretch. Be aware of your body and surroundings. Last, allow your eyes to open gently in their own time. If it's bright where you are, you can put your palms over your eyes.

Nuggets

Visualisation or Imagination (VI) can lead to many distractions. Apply the option of One Breath meditation to settle your mind.

Remember (from the chapter on *Myth: I Cannot Visualise*), there doesn't need to be any *visual* elements. You use the story from the guided VI to *nudge* your imagination.

Always use minimal effort to *visualise* anything. Focus instead on being *aware* of the story elements that *pop into your head*, or the *feelings* that arise.

On the app, there is a VI to help with the Authentic Attitude (AA) of kindness. It acts to lift your spirits and creates a better internal environment for therapeutic meditation. The one above is also on the app as an audio.

I've also added simple exercises to enhance your visualisation capabilities to the app (use the code in the Resources chapter).

None of these resources to help you meditate are of any use if you don't have time to meditate. Unless having no time to meditate is a myth?

15

Myth: I Don't Have Enough Time to Meditate

IN OUR SOCIETY, THIS is big. "With everything I have to do in my day, I cannot possibly find twenty minutes to sit down and do nothing!"

Meditation is doing nothing, or being self-indulgent, is a myth I discussed earlier. The "not enough time" issue can persist even if we have no other myths. Until you realise why it isn't true.

Meditation is incredibly refreshing for your body and mind. People notice, when they stick to their meditation routine, they can achieve more while doing less. They let go of pushing hard to accomplish their goals (creating stress). Instead, they achieve more because of being *in the flow* more often.

Stress in your body can speed up the ageing process and give you the subjective feeling that you are "running out of time." While meditating, your breathing and heart rate slow down, your blood pressure lowers, and your body lets go of stress hormones and chemicals.

When you use your time wisely to meditate regularly, you have more time.

Do You Have Thirty Seconds?

When teaching a course, I ask, "How long does it take to meditate?" Most answers vary between five to twenty minutes. The answer is under thirty seconds.

Under thirty seconds! How does that work?

Check the time, then focus your attention on the breath – either at the nostrils or the tummy. Recheck the time as soon as you can feel either:

- The rise and fall of the belly.

- Coolness as the air passes by your nostrils on an in-breath.

- The warmth of the air as you exhale.

- Any pressure as the air passes in or out of the nostrils.

You are meditating as soon as you decide to meditate and notice the object of meditation (the breath). The rest is staying with the object, as described in the chapter on EA.

Do You have Twenty Minutes?

Because of the natural rhythm of brain and body functions, the ideal time is eighteen to twenty-four minutes. Personally, I've noticed my rhythm is at the shorter end of the range. Everything about me is short – right down to the short socks I wear – so no surprise there.

Your natural rhythm could be twenty minutes or longer. Experiment to find out. Allow for your natural rhythm to change over time.

For me, the first meditation of the day was hard to get into. Instead of prolonging the angst, I'd get up at the twenty minute mark. Once refreshed, my second meditation is more relaxed, yet less distracted, and two or three times longer.

Occasionally, the first meditation was the best of that day. See the discussion on meditation being like a game of snakes and ladders in the chapter, *Myth: You Never Fall Back*.

Any amount of time – from three seconds up – is better than none. If you feel your schedule is too packed, I encourage you to <u>not</u> talk yourself out of meditating. Nor because it's not a *perfect* time, it's a bit late, or you feel sleepy (see the section on this in the FAQ, Chapter 19).

My Mind Is Too Busy

If you have a busy mind, you will have to do a meditation designed to *calm the mind*. Not all forms of meditation do this. It is best to learn under competent guidance. Although the instructions seem straightforward, there are many nuances to navigate. A body relaxation, then focusing on the breath, can calm your mind.

Remember, to expect your thoughts to become still is going to create tension you do not need or want. You can't stop or control your thoughts, but you *can* decide how much of your focus and attention to give them. That's assuming you do not have an energy imbalance (as described in the chapter on the *Myth: Try Hard To Succeed*).

I'm Too Stressed to Meditate

A busy mind can be a symptom of stress. I have a non-meditation process I use with clients to help them get beyond their *busy and stressed mind*. They can then quickly take advantage of meditation – without the painful struggle. I recommend the *Melt Stress Within Minutes* protocol to stressed clients (it is on the app).

Engrossed Attention (EA) – especially on the feeling of relaxation from Restful Absorption (RA) – is excellent for stress reduction. Add the first couple of Authentic Attitudes (AA), and you have a recipe for quick, therapeutic change.

Informal techniques can help the busy mind to relax. For example, a breathing technique may help. Sometimes, nothing seems to work. But if you check closely, you will find things have shifted. Maybe not to the extent you'd like.

Let's say your mind is whirring like a big tornado and you do a practice to subdue it. The result is, you are now dealing with a *small* tornado. However, it can appear as if nothing changed. Your mind is still a tornado!

A big tornado to a small tornado is a definite shift in the right direction — and without using drugs, lots of time, or cost.

You also do not need:

- To be in a special state before you meditate.

- To de-stress before doing the One Breath meditation.

In rare cases (specifically when there is an energy imbalance), I tell a student to stop meditating and do informal practices instead. Only for a little while.

In most cases, I am saying to do more meditation, despite not being in the mood, or maybe feeling too stressed.

The Desire to Do

Part of the reason *informal* practices are so popular is because it directs you to *do* something other than meditate. The breath is being controlled. You're walking in nature. Tai chi or yoga are what you are doing. You are chanting affirmations. There are parts of you that are far more comfortable doing something – anything.

Informal practice is wonderful. The distinction is that you can only become an IntrAnaut through *formal* practice. Formal practice can take your attempts at self-therapy to a new level. Use every technique available as a preparation for meditation, but do not neglect formal practice. That's where the magic lies.

16

Question or Introspect (QI)

THE QUESTIONS YOU ASK about life have a profound effect on what you do and where you end up. In meditation, your questions direct your attention, but can also direct your life.

Questions can draw out your intuitive faculties. Asking philosophical questions will exercise the opening of your mind at the level of your intuition and beyond. For example, such questions as "Who am I?" or "What is life?"

In this type of meditation, the goal is <u>not</u> to *think* of an answer. You're giving your vast mind an opportunity to show you what you need to know. However, don't just accept the first *answer* that pops into your head. Your deeper mind will assume your thirst for knowledge has been quenched.

Do not accept the first answer. What do you do instead?

You say "That's interesting, I wonder if there is more to this?" and ask your question again. Now you might get a different *answer*.

If you are actively looking, or seeking, an *answer* to your question, you are no longer meditating. You are thinking, or you are creating tension. As with Visualisation or Imagination (VI) style meditations, you nudge (ask questions), then let go, and see what comes up.

Once you ask your question, you let go. The analogy is a boomerang. Stay where you are so you can catch it when it returns. You don't follow it. You don't go hunting for it. There are questions, but no *hunting for answers*.

If you don't seek an answer to a question, what do you do instead?

Use Restful Absorption (RA) and surrender. Deeply relax, but stay awake to whatever you might receive. Occasionally, you can re-establish the question, if:

- You've received an answer.

- Your mind has gone foggy, or become sleepy.

- You forget what you're doing (boredom?).

- You have had to increase your energy by adding an Authentic Attitude (AA), or an informal practice.

What is the motivation behind your questions?

A big factor in the level of insight you attain is your motivation for finding out where your enquiry will lead. You are not just seeking an answer – you want to know the truth. You want to be consciously aware of what you know at the deepest levels of your mind.

Question or Introspect (QI) opens up your mind for deeper insight. In this sense, *opens up* is like opening an apple to find the seeds inside.

QI has a connection with the beginner's mind. That is curiosity. We could ask ourselves, "What am I missing in relation to this?", or "What more is there to know, feel, sense?" For example, when your intention is to focus on the breath, add curiosity. Ask with interest, "What are the sensations associated with the breath?", and "Can I be aware of more?"

Introspect

Introspection comes into play specifically with Question or Introspect (QI) style meditations and works in the background for all other meditations.

Introspection is an awareness outside of your Intentional Awareness (IA) and works closely with your questioning self. It's a slightly different kind of awareness. QI is a peripheral awareness, outside of your conscious awareness. Whereas, IA is a deliberately observed, conscious awareness.

Introspection is a peripheral attention to what else is going on. It asks, "Is there something else you can pay attention to?" Are you still paying attention? Are you still engaged in your intention?

Introspection has you, along with your memory, do a "check in" on things. While you focus on the details of the sensations of the breath, introspection is aware of the length of the breath. Introspection may ask, "What about the length of the breath?" so your focus turns to the length of the breath. You thereby bring your peripheral awareness of your breath into conscious awareness. You now know the answer to that question because introspection has brought it into your conscious awareness.

Contemplation Is QI

If someone says, "Meditation and prayer are the same", they often mean the Questions or Introspect (QI) sphere of meditation. In Buddhism, there are *contemplation* style meditations.

The contemplation of logical arguments comes under QI in this framework. It can take the form of considering statements that lead you to a conclusion, upon which you rest your focus. An example is the meditation below, which can help to re-balance your mind if you have inaccurate thoughts that undermine your self-esteem.

When using logic to come to a conclusion, or feeling, there are hidden questions. Is it true? Where does this line of enquiry lead? How do I feel about the conclusion?

Treat logical arguments during meditation in the same way as you would questions (see above). Only as prompts for your intuition (right brain insights); not to analyse, evaluate, or compare (left brain thinking).

Meditation: Am I Good?

The meditation below is an example of a reflective meditation using logical arguments to answer the question, "Am I good?"

Your introspection gathers the relevant information or feelings from beyond your awareness. The more you relax, the deeper your introspection can go to fetch a response. You may notice the response is not a verbal *answer*, but mostly a feeling.

Before you do this meditation, there are two bits of preparation.

- List on a sheet of paper, every skill you have from every part of your life (not just thoughs on your CV).

- List the *good* qualities you have displayed, or felt, at any time in your life (fill a sheet of paper, or more).

Now into the meditation.

1. Get yourself comfortable – sitting, standing, or lying – with your eyes open or closed, and relax.

2. Scan your body for tension. If you feel any, release it, let it go, and fully relax the muscles in that area.

3. Use the One Breath meditation at the belly until the activity of your mind reduces. It is important to use any method that works for you to relax your body and quieten the mind.

4. Silently list the skills you have. Read your list if you need to.

5. Contemplate: "Any skill I have learned is still a part of me now, even if I feel I cannot recall every part of how to do it."

6. Contemplate: "It would simply take a little revision to rekindle any skill I once had."

7. Contemplate: "The important thing is, I have or had that ability."

8. Pause into the relaxation and focus on the breath. Surrender to the space created for insights or feelings to arise.

9. Focus on the feeling created by the conclusion (if positive).*

10. List the *good* qualities you have displayed or felt at any time in your life. Your written list will help.

11. Contemplate: "Any *good* quality I have expressed or experienced – even just once – *must* be a part of me."

12. Contemplate: "Any *good* quality I have can grow, no matter how small it seems to be."

13. Contemplate: "The important thing is, I have that quality. It is a part of what makes me, me."

14. Pause and surrender to the space created for insights or feelings to arise.

15. Focus on the feeling created by the conclusion (if positive).*

16. If your eyes are shut, allow them to open gently in their own time. If it's bright, you can put your palms over your eyes for extra gentleness.

* If depressed, this meditation could help a lot. For some, their mind could be so distressed it sabotages the process. Use

other meditation styles until you can do this one with a positive outcome. Then it will boost your recovery.

Nuggets

You will notice, from the above (*), not every meditation is suitable for everyone at every stage of life. That's one reason for this book. I want to give you enough guidance, so if one style doesn't suit you now, then you can still meditate using another form of meditation.

It could be that this meditation will work amazingly well immediately after another meditation. Maybe one that has you feeling good, or reduces your stress.

This is not a list of affirmations. It is a list of accurate statements: in this case, of skills and qualities you already have. The resulting conclusion or feelings arise naturally (unless distorted by sabotaging thoughts).

You do not *create* the positive feelings, but you *focus* on them once they appear. Notice the nuance here: it is *not* positive thinking, or deliberately changing your state. Yet meditation changes you.

Questions lead you to introspect. There is no introspection without an intention or question.

I Highly Recommend Stacking

Two ways you can stack the odds in your favour:

1. Add more and more layers of appreciation (or any Authentic Attitude (AA) you can access), or good qualities (as in the above meditation), etc.

2. Use more than one process or technique in meditation to get a result.

On my retreats, participants gain altitude with their practice and *stack* the bliss. We use that joy with Engrossed Attention (EA) to *stack* processes in healing meditations. As an example, we may stack the following in one meditation to drop a distorted, limiting belief:

- Stacking peace, openness, and joy.
- The Release Technique by Lester Levenson.
- The Work by Byron Katie.
- NLP techniques.
- We then reinforce the melting of your beliefs using your True Nature.

That web of beliefs holding you back doesn't have a chance! Especially when we stack this meditation, plus other supporting practices, within the hugely favourable setting of a retreat.

Retreats produce quantum leaps in your personal evolution.

Some people believe that to learn meditation at one level means we will never need to go back to that level. This kind of stacking – of levels of progress – will always fall down (at least till you become a qualified intrAnaut).

Read on to discover why meditation training can be like a game of snakes and ladders.

17

Myth: You Can Never Fall Back

A MEDITATION PRACTICE LEADS to deeper states, so you never go back to battling a busy mind. Hmm, not really: at least not till you're a master intrAnaut. Before you get there, the route up the mountain could feel as if there is as many troughs as there are peaks.

An adept in meditation can have a busy mind. They are an intrAnaut because they have stopped struggling, done their time in meditation, and never given up on the *process*.

I talk about meditation as a *process*, as you saw in the chapter, *Myth: Try Hard To Succeed*. You don't have to worry about the goal being achieved. That creates stress. Instead, your task is to meditate (without expectations) and meditate some more. By approaching it this way, you give your mind and body the chance to *process your stress*. This leads to you experiencing peaceful states (but not all the time).

Success Ladder or Snake?

You've read about the bubbles of stress that can produce uncomfortable feelings in your body. The same stress-releasing process often creates distractions, which may get you feeling frustrated at your lack of progress. In fact, you are making headway in your release of accumulated stress. Over time, the uncomfortable feelings will subside.

Only a few sessions of meditation will often result in sessions where the tension subsides. You get to experience various forms of peace, quiet, OK-ness, feeling relaxed, or maybe contented. Not every session, not the whole of a session, but glimpses that will grow as you continue your practice.

You cannot always define what stage you are at. Sometimes you will experience a spike of altitude, so you jump a stage or two. A wave of contentment, or love, or bliss may take you to new heights. You could have a major insight of wisdom, or your cocoon keeps you pinned to your object of meditation for an hour. Yet, the next meditation has you distracted for an hour.

How is meditation like the game of snakes and ladders?[1]

=|=|=|=|= You could land on a ladder and soar to the highs of Restful Absorption (RA) quickly and easily. Within the cocoon, you feel comfortable, contented, and clear of mental disturbance.

~~~~<>< No matter how many levels of the game you go up, you could land on a snake (i.e., a stressful situation). You slide back down so it feels as if you're distracted, agitated, and frustrated.

If you can slide back down again, is it worth doing?

Yes! Just three (of many) reasons:

1. Meditation will help you manage the new stressful situation better than before you were meditating.

2. You get to go up a ladder and see life from a different perspective.

3. Even if you land on a snake, it doesn't take long to get back onto another ladder – yippee!

---

1. Unsure what I mean by a game of Snakes and Ladders? See it on Wikipedia - https://en.wikipedia.org/wiki/Snakes_and_ladders

Unfortunately, you cannot predict how the next meditation session will go – up or down. Within a series of sessions, there will be patches where your progress falls apart. It may feel as if you have gone back to the start. These are the times when it's handy to have a friend who is an experienced meditator (or even better, a competent teacher).

Why is thinking of it as a game of Snakes And Ladders useful?

People think of gaining progress as a straight line. You start at the beginning and move upward toward your goal. Descriptions of progress in meditation seem to show a straight line of forward movement. In reality, it doesn't work that way. There will be periods where your progress seems to have dissolved into nothing.

The point is, the road to becoming an intrAnaut is bumpy (possibly frustrating). Persistence is needed to get the most from your practice. Your meditations will go through muddy patches and feel difficult. But you will make headway even when it doesn't feel like it.

Long-term meditators – who have had a regular practice (not every day) for years – say they have far more good days than bad. They experience far more happiness and contentment than they did before meditating. They also have more enjoyable meditation experiences. This is mostly because of the release of accumulated stress. Less accumulated stress means there is a larger capacity to deal with new stresses.

Expectations and the Real Benefit of Meditation

It is not just deep peace people expect to experience in their first few attempts at meditation. Some people have read meditation can lead to experiencing many phenomena. They've heard people gain visions, bliss, or attain enlightenment. They then expect similar experiences. These are things you could work toward. However, not every type of meditation will take you there.

Connecting with calmness is not far away. There are also a variety of wonderful experiences you can encounter when you meditate, including feelings of bliss and oneness. These aren't the purpose of the practice at the beginning. Making them into an expectation will create a subtle tension that gets in the way.

The real benefit of meditation is the change in your experience of the world in your daily life.

When regular meditators get up from their meditation, they bring the benefits received from their practice with them. This allows them to be more creative, kind, emotionally balanced, and loving toward themselves and others. There are plenty of mindfulness and other informal practices you can do in your daily life, but meditation strengthens your ability to use them.

Goal versus Experiment

The purpose of meditation says you can use it to help you achieve your goals. That doesn't mean you should engage in meditation as a goal-setting exercise. "My goal with this meditation is to feel profound peace, and by the end of tomorrow's meditation, my goal is to be enlightened." That's a recipe for disappointment.

Instead, approach your meditation as an experiment.

How do you approach an experiment?

1. Choose the boundaries of your test by deciding on your intentions. For example, maybe you intend to "Relax, let go, be as conscious as I can – with few-to-no thoughts about what to expect."

2. Observe with an open mind and curiosity (the beginner's mind).

3. Have a keen interest in the results – whatever they may look like – without labelling them good or bad.

Please note: intentions differ from goals:

- Goals are future-based and have a pre-planned result.

- Intentions are of the present moment, relating to a direction you wish to explore.

Is there a sphere of meditation where progress may appear linear as you get familiar with it?

For most forms of meditation, there are recognisable stages of progress toward mastery. If you attempt to push yourself along, in the middle-to-later stages, you will definitely fall back. By pushing, you will create an energy imbalance. Not in the beginning stages, but as your body-mind system becomes refined.

The advice you're receiving is not just about saving you from frustration and disappointment. What would be the point of purifying your body-mind and gaining all the benefits from that, just to wreck it by pushing?

I've said many times up till now:

- Meditation is exclusively of the mind.

- A principle of meditation is rest, which includes the stillness of your body.

- Controlling your body, including the breath, is not meditation.

Therefore, how can vocalising sounds in the syllables of a mantra, possibly be meditation? Go to the next chapter to discover the nuances of meditation with sound.

18

Mantra or Invocation (MI)

In the beginning was sound

PSYCHOLOGISTS TELL US: THE thoughts (words) we hear repeatedly have a dramatic effect on how we perceive ourselves.

If you are musically inclined, Mantra or Invocation (MI) can be the easiest way to get into meditation.

By now, you might expect me to say, "The word *mantra* has various definitions." You'd be right. Nowadays, the term is used to mean *a phrase you repeat*.

The other day, I was chatting to a friend about *allowing miracles to happen in your life*. I heard myself say, "*Dispense with Dis-belief* is my new mantra." In this context, I was using the Western, social definition of the term.

In the context of meditation, however, a mantra is:

> A set of syllables used to resonate with specific frequencies. They may not be words.

What do I mean by resonate with specific frequencies?

By turning your radio dial to a specific frequency, you can tune in to the channel you want to listen to. The word, *resonate*, means to be *in tune with*, or *connect with*.

What are you resonating with or tuning in to?

If you are a devout atheist, you may desire to tune-out at this point. Or read on to get an idea of how to use Mantra or Invocation (MI) *without* religion.

Invocation

The *specific frequencies* are what you invoke through your Mantra or Invocation (MI). In ancient times, people could connect with their deepest principles through meditation. Later, individuals who personified those principles became saints. Storytellers made them into mythological beings, or deities.

The people most likely to be seen as god-like, were the original IntrAnauts, because of the purification process that occurs through meditation.

For example, for compassion, I'd recommend the mantra of the Compassion Buddha "Om Mani Padme Hum." The Compassion Buddha is not a deity, but an awakened person who left behind a calling card (a mantra).

For over two thousand years, people have invoked the essence of compassion through his mantra. Download the app for examples of mantras, including "Om Mani Padme Hum."

Many of the Mantra or Invocations (MI) are directed toward deities, or awakened masters. But if you look past the outward symbolic representation, you find the innate principles of your mind. These principles — such as peace, love, compassion, wisdom, etc. — are archetypes from the deepest reaches of your mind.

In the chapter on the Authentic Attitudes (AA), I have a diagram with clouds on one side and the sun on the other. As you become an IntrAnaut, meditation clears away the clouds, as the distorted minds caused by stress evaporate.

Have you ever seen the sun shine through a hole in the clouds? Meditation can create those holes long before you become an IntrAnaut.

Mantra or Invocation (MI) is also designed to create a hole in the clouds. Attempting to shine the deepest parts of your mind onto you and your distorted minds.

MI does this by attempting to tune in to a channel that's well established (a wide bandwidth). If you do not know the exact frequency, the easiest way is to piggyback off the nearest channel you have available. This will often be that of a so-called deity.

I'm not suggesting you just find any mantra from any religion. You should do your research. Ask yourself if the mantra is inviting the principles – such as peace, love, compassion, wisdom – you want to embody?

Devotional

The part of Buddhism I had the most difficulty with was the devotional practitioners. For me, I want to know the Truth and the essence of who and what I am.

This searching originally began as an interest in our human potential. I had no interest in turning that into a religious pursuit. Especially what I saw as Buddhism's practical methods to awaken our ultimate potential.

Yet, there are Buddhists who display what I thought were sycophantic attitudes. Their devotion to their teachers and Buddha felt at odds with the logic and precision of the teachings. Admittedly, some teachings promoted devotional behaviour. But I could dismiss these as needless add-ons designed to keep the religion alive.

For me, my biggest problem with devotional practice was that it seemed to involve blind faith.

Recently, my view has opened up to new possibilities. For many people, I now believe a devotional attitude can act as a powerful fuel for awakening their innate potentials. Possibly, those who could benefit the most are those with the greatest resistance.

I'm not saying devotion to a teacher is a substitute for working toward becoming an intrAnaut. In fact, there are a dozen caveats I'd suggest, but that discussion is for another time.

Mantra or Invocation (MI) is right for you if you can fall in love with the Truth (even if it is still abstract to you), your practice, and the potential of where the teachings will take you.

Despite my doubts because of the possible religious connection, I've attended two three-month silent retreats where a mantra was the main meditation.

One was a three-month purification retreat, where the primary practice was a 100-syllable mantra. Although the retreat was in silence, we'd chant for a few minutes at the beginning of the 60-90 minute mantra sessions.

Chanting Is the Informal Practice of Mantra

Music (audio) can have an emotional impact. If you love music and harmony, you may be able to open to the devotional aspect that makes MI special. The hard part is to let go of making the sounds externally.

A Mantra or Invocation (MI) is repeated mentally. When sung as a chant, it is an *informal* practice.

Chanting is a physical, vocal activity. However, you can chant silently within your mind. As you let go of controlling the vocal cords, it draws you deeper into the expanse of your mind.

My Old Friend, Mantra

Here is a bit from *The Joy of Living: Unlocking the Secret and Science of Happiness*, by Yongey Mingyur Rinpoche. He tells us how MI is actually a mental recitation, but you can start the practice verbally. I've added the *emphasis*.

Mantra meditation is a very powerful technique that not only cultivates clear awareness, but also, through the potency of syllables that have been recited by enlightened masters for thousands of years, clears away layers of mental obscuration and increases our capacity to benefit ourselves and others. This connection may be hard to accept at first; it seems too much like magic. It might be easier to think of mantric syllables as sound waves that perpetuate through space for thousands, perhaps millions, of years.

In mantra meditation, the focus of your attention is on the *mental recitation* of a certain set of syllables that appear to have a direct effect on calming and clearing the mind. For this exercise, we'll use a very simple set of three syllables that make up the most basic of all mantras: OM AH HUNG.

OM represents the lucid, distinctive, perceptual aspect of experience; AH represents the empty, or inherently open, aspect; while HUNG represents the union of distinctive appearance and the inherently empty nature of the appearance.

You can *start by reciting the mantra aloud, and then gradually slip into a more internal form of mental recitation.* The important thing is to continue *reciting the mantra mentally* for about three minutes, and then just let your mind rest, alternating between recitation and resting for as long as you can. Whether you feel the effects immediately or not, you've set something in motion. That "something" is the freedom of your mind.

Meditation: "Om"

Several times, when I've mentioned I meditate, the response has been "Oh, you Ommm!" Most mantras from the East have the "Om" syllable at the beginning, but you can also use it on its own. Here is your easy way to get into Mantra or Invocation (MI), using "Om":

1. Get yourself comfortable. Sitting on a chair, standing, or lying. With your eyes open or closed, relax.

2. Start by taking a deep breath in. On the out-breath, vocalise the syllable "Ahh", like a sigh from the back of your throat.

3. About a third of the way through your exhale, gradually change the sound to an "Au". When I do this, my mouth goes from being wide for the "Ahh" toward a shut mouth, and the noise naturally changes.

4. At around the three-quarters mark, change the vocal so it is an "mmm" before the end of the breath. Your mouth is now closed.

5. Take another deep breath in and repeat the vocals on the exhale.

6. Be aware of the sensations within your body as you chant.

7. Let go of the three separate syllables and allow them to melt into each other. Be aware of how your vocals change — not only as described above, but also the tones, pitch, and length of each segment.

8. When you feel comfortable with the flow of the chanting, let go of the chanting. Repeat the mantra in your head for about three minutes.

9. After about three minutes of mantra, rest. Notice how your body and mind feel. Rest some more.

10. As you continue with your MI, notice if you are connecting the internal (imaginary) sound with your mouth or throat. Gently let go of any connection to anything physical, including your breathing. Gently nudge until your MI is completely mental, then experiment with pitch, tone, rhythm, etc., until you feel comfortable and fully relaxed.

11. Extend the Restful Absorption (RA) between your three minutes of MI.

12. If your eyes were shut, allow them to open gently in their own time. If it's bright, you can put your palms over your eyes for extra gentleness.

Nuggets

Don't want to disturb your neighbours with your tone-deaf attempts to meditate with a mantra? You can do all this silently by imagining you can hear the sounds in your mind.

Imagine you are making the sounds. Feel your mouth move as you do, if that helps. Let go of the vocal cords bit by bit until you can hear the sounds without them.

Finding it hard to let go of the vocal cords?

If you enjoy chanting, then letting go of the physical side of creating sounds can seem weird. Here are some tips. Use any, or as many, that help:

- Next time you notice you're talking in your head, get that voice to say the mantra.

- Emotionally celebrate (using the AA of appreciation, etc.), each time you can do a mantra mentally.

1. Remember a character on a TV show you watch. Remember how they sound. Imagine them saying the mantra.

2. Remember other characters and get each one to say the mantra. Line them up, saying the mantra, one by one.

3. In addition to the above, or just after, imagine a choir (or group of angelic beings) chanting the mantra.

- Imagine the sound of the mantra filling your body. Remember, VI is not to be held. It is a nudge that can be vague and fleeting.

When you work on the mind-technologies of RA, EA and AA, your MI practice becomes a completely different experience. There are many subtle aspects of MI the vast majority of people have never come across.

You have now explored all seven of the mind-technologies that make up meditation. Yet, people can still have a lot of questions — so PART THREE starts with a chapter on *Frequently Asked Questions*. More gems!

PART THREE - Next Steps

Resources and FAQs

19

Frequently Asked Questions

THERE ARE MANY MYTHS surrounding meditation. For instance, almost every photograph used to show meditation has people cross-legged with their knees up. Buddhist monks and nuns do not teach you to sit in this way.

Those photos often show people with their hands on their knees, with thumb and finger touching. They use this finger-touching in Kundalini Yoga, but not in Buddhism.

In this chapter, I advise what I consider are the essentials to get started with meditation.

Posture – Must I Sit Cross-legged?

You can sit on a chair, stand, or lie down. A reasonably straight back is important. Even more important is to be comfortable, but not slouched.

Some people think being relaxed means to slump into an armchair. However, for meditation, this is unsuitable. It's best to sit with your spine lengthened and naturally taking the weight of your body. If this is painful (not just uncomfortable because you're unfamiliar with sitting in this position), you can sit with your back resting on the upright of a chair.

Want to sit cross-legged?

The correct sitting posture, if you want to sit cross-legged on a mat, is to have your bottom higher than your knees. If you cannot sit cross-legged on the floor with your thighs flat on the mat, then you need to be sitting on a cushion – with your calves on the floor. To sit cross-legged, check the instructions on the app (find the QR code on the page at the end of the chapter, *Resources and What Next?*).

Where do I put my hands?

When on a chair, place your hands on your lap to rest in a comfortable position. One hand on top of the other (palms facing up) is convenient for most people. In this position, you do not have to wonder if a hand is slipping or moving.

When sitting cross-legged, I rest my hands on a fold in my jumper, below my naval. Some people place a small cushion on their lap to rest their hands. You can also use a cushion if you're sitting on a chair.

The reason for using a cushion (or fold in your clothing) is so your arms are away from your body. Have your elbows pointing out to the sides so you ventilate your armpits. It can help you feel as if you have room to breathe.

When lying or sitting, make sure your thighs are slightly apart for the same reason.

Thumbs touching?

Now we are getting into the dynamics of energy circulation. It is *not essential* to have your thumbs touching. If it is comfortable, go ahead. A monk taught me to have my thumbs *almost* touching.

If your teacher tells you to have your hands in this way, ask: why? It is best to know, because that knowledge will add power to your practice.

Index finger touching the thumb?

In many photos of meditators, you see them with their forefinger touching the thumb. *This is not essential.* The same caveat applies here as the one for your thumbs touching.

Prefer to lie down to meditate?

If you fall asleep when meditating lying down, you need to sit up for meditation. Unless you specifically want to sleep – but you still need to be cautious because only meditating yourself to sleep can cause you to habituate sleep. This will make it harder to meditate without falling asleep. If you can meditate (and stay awake) while lying down, there is no problem.

What about my head and tongue?

Rest your tongue on the top palate or behind your teeth, if that feels comfortable. This helps you breathe through your nose.

Lift the top of your head (the crown). This should draw your jaw in toward your throat (just a little) and lengthen your spine.

None of the posture adjustments are essential. However, they can help you stay awake and comfortable if meditating for any length of time.

Where Can I Meditate – Do I Need a Special Room?

You can meditate almost anywhere.

At first, you may wish to sit somewhere quiet. It doesn't need to be peaceful to meditate. Meditating in nature is great. However, with all the birds chirping away in the woods, it is not silent.

You can use any sounds that distract you as a useful practice: to trigger you to bring your attention back to your meditation object (e.g., the breath).

Somewhere you will not be disturbed while you meditate is ideal. Again, it is not a requirement. People meditate in busy family homes (sometimes sitting in the bathroom). Others meditate on the train or bus.

I talked to a guy who said he was too nervous to meditate on the bus, like I do. My suggestion was to try it with his eyes half-open, looking down but unfocused. He could instantly be aware of anyone approaching. And have his attention on the breath. There would be plenty of mind wandering (and distraction), but also meditation.

Since you take all the equipment with you wherever you go, you can relax and meditate almost anywhere.

Many people find it useful to wear headphones. They use music without words to help them focus inward.

Can I Eat and Drink Before Meditation?

Hydration is important, so drink plenty of water before you sit down to meditate. If you haven't hydrated beforehand, have some water by your side when meditating.

We were told off by a monk for having water bottles by our sides during sessions. Therefore, on retreat, drink between sessions.

Meditating while hungry can distract you as your mind wanders to your tummy to check out the pangs. It is *ideal* to have eaten within the last two to four hours. A light meal over an hour before is the *ideal*.

The *ideals* are irrelevant if you fast regularly or you are an experienced meditator.

Many meditators report that caffeine prior to meditating can get them too stimulated so their minds become distracted. Others say sugary drinks or foods can have the same effect. The same with spicy foods or alcohol.

Not everyone is alike, so experiment with this to see where your tolerances lie.

People naturally feel sluggish after a big meal. The more stodgy the meal, the more heavy you may feel. This could get you feeling sleepy during meditation, so you struggle to stay awake.

What Do I Need to Wear?

Loose clothing is ideal, but not a requirement. I sometimes wear a shirt and suit trousers when I teach meditation to show students you don't need to dress like a hippy to meditate. Just as you are, you don't need special clothing.

Loosen your belt if it is restricting your breathing. Take off your shoes if they feel tight. The key criteria are to feel comfortable and able to rest your muscles.

It is a valid Intentional Awareness (IA) *informal* practice to notice the difference in how it feels to be wearing each piece of clothing from your wardrobe.

How Long Must I Meditate For?

Your meditation may last as long as you have the time or inclination to meditate. You know, from the chapter on EA (chapter 9), it can take just One Breath to meditate.

For best results, how long is best?

If you can only do five minutes, that's better than thirty seconds and puts you beyond the beginner. Ten minutes is better than five and will have you reaping the benefits faster.

The ideal time is eighteen to twenty-four minutes – as I describe in the chapter, *Myth: I Don't Have Enough Time To Meditate*. As a beginner, you can use this natural cycle to come out feeling refreshed and at ease.

Do people meditate for longer than twenty-four minutes?

Although there is a natural rhythm, you can notice you're coming out of meditation and dive straight back in.

For me, the rhythm would tell me how long I'd been in meditation. Each time I felt myself surfacing, I'd know I'd been meditating for another twenty minutes.

At those times when I was struggling, it would give me the natural prompt to have a break.

When Is The Best Time to Meditate?

Optimum times are when you are most wide awake, but often those times are taken up by other activities. Choose convenient times for you. It's better to have a practice that's sluggish or distracted than no practice at all. If you can only meditate during the least optimum times, by meditating, you will find these periods become less disturbing.

- Any time is a good time to meditate (unless you are moving, in which case it will be an *Informal* practice).

Two times spring to mind as excellent times to meditate:

- First thing in the morning, when you wake up, sit up in bed and meditate. If you, like me, are too sleepy, have a cold shower first.

- When you go back to bed in the evening, meditate before you go to sleep.

Less optimum times to meditate (but it may be still OK):

- Immediately after a meal.

- When you are exhausted.

Please do not make these into rules so as to dump meditation because they are the only times you have available.

Falling Asleep When Meditating

We need to recognise most people have a sleep deficit. Getting the balance between struggling to stay awake when resting in meditation and falling asleep because of a sleep deficiency is probably the hardest thing about meditation.

If the only chance you get is when you go to bed (or exhausted), you are still meditating. Use it to help you have a healthy sleep for now. Have the intention that at some point, *soon*, you will give yourself a 30+ second break during the day whenever you can. It will fall into place, eventually.

Use Meditation to Get to Sleep

Doing a meditation emphasising absorption is an excellent way to get some zzzzz. However, I'd advise you also meditate at another time so you can gain the full benefits.

> Intend to *let go of the meditation* and *intend to sleep* as soon as you feel the effects of slumber.

Keep in mind the caution about *only* meditating yourself to sleep. It can become a habit and make it harder to meditate without falling asleep.

How Often Do I Need to Meditate?

At minimum once per week or fortnight, at a meditation class/group/drop-in. If you can, or have a soundtrack to guide you, once per day is excellent. Twice per day is ideal.

There is no limit to how often you meditate as long as you are not giving up your other daily activities to *blank your mind*. To *blank your mind* is not the intention or purpose of meditation. See the *Myth: I Cannot Meditate* for more details on the seduction of a blank mind.

You can go on a retreat when you are ready to extend your practice.

If you join the app, I will invite you to the next (FREE) *5-Day Meditation Challenge.* During the challenge, I will show you how to do the One Breath meditation and extend it. This has you meditating many times a day – which helps you get into your longer meditations.

My Mind Has Become Hyper Since Meditating!!!!!

One problem I see often is that people think their mind has become hyper since meditating. This happens because they are now noticing a level of distracting thoughts and emotions that were previously hidden.

The loudness of the up-front thinking had kept it hidden, and they hadn't decided to be conscious to this level before. Those *new* thoughts <u>were there the whole time</u> but meditating has helped you become aware of it!

It does appear that the stress-release is front-loaded. Add, greater awareness, to stress release (creating distracting thoughts), and you can see how it could appear that you're getting worse at meditation.

At first, people experience a lot of distraction in their meditations as they release a lot of stress. Later, the frustrations ease as the meditation processes deeper levels of stress. To get past the hump, use the Authentic Attitudes (AA).

I also recommend using informal practices, as well as meditation, to help with releasing stress.

20

Get into the Habit

FOR MANY, HOW TO meditate isn't that difficult. What is, is getting into the habit. This chapter is essential reading for anyone who finds it hard to get into the habit.

Meditation can be extremely easy. The benefits of any sphere of meditation can be life-changing.

Yet, most people fall at the first hurdle. They cannot get into the habit of meditating. Let's change that. As a coach, I support clients to develop new habits. Often it is one of the most important things I do for them. I really appreciate the way James Clear has laid out the process in his books, *Atomic Habits* and the *Workbook for James Clear's Atomic Habits*.

What is involved in the James Clear's process?

Four Steps to Building Good Habits

1. Cue. You see or hear a trigger, which reminds you of the reward.

2. Craving. You want the reward.

3. Response. You respond by engaging in the behaviour (the habit).

4. Reward. What your behaviour (your habit) gives you that makes it all worthwhile.

The *rewards* are the benefits of meditation, such as reduced stress. *Response* is the act of meditating (your habit). The craving is your desire to meditate because you know how wonderful it is. *Cue* is the time, place, or signal you decided will trigger your habit of meditation.

How might that look in practice?

1. Cue. You decide to use the One Breath meditation every time you *rest from staring at the screen* (Health and Safety advice is to come away from your screen at least once per hour). You decide to meditate for at least five minutes *on the way home from work* – either on the public transport (with headphones), or park your car somewhere safe.

2. Craving. You have books to read about meditation masters to inspire you. You have notes about the benefits of meditation published by scientists.

3. Response. Refuse to do anything else until you have had your One Breath meditation. You make sure your phone can not disturb your five minutes.

4. Reward. Decide to bring any calmness you experience in meditation out into your life. Congratulate yourself, no matter how the meditation *seems* to go. Remind yourself of the bubbles of stress you have released (especially if you felt distracted). You pay attention to how you feel before and after meditation, maybe using the 1—10 scale. The 1—10 scale is for how agitated, stressed, or anxious you feel. Ten means you feel panicky, whereas one means you feel at rest, calm, and content.

We are all different, with different lives, so I cannot tell you exactly what is best for you. Below is some guidance, so you can create a plan that fits you and your life. But what are the things that stop you from being successful with your new meditation habit? Once you identify these hurdles, you can make better plans for creating your new habit.

Problems with Creating New Habits

1. The *cue* is not obvious, clear, or stable.

2. The *craving* is not strong enough.

3. The *response* is not restricted, so you choose other options.

4. The *reward* is not clear.

Now you know what can go wrong, the way forward is obvious – do the opposite. James Clear has Four Rules.

Four Rules of Behaviour Change

1. Cue. Make the reminder obvious. E.g., phone alerts, schedule time in your diary, or add meditation to the start or end of another activity.

2. Craving. Make the reward attractive. E.g., put up quotes on the benefits of meditation, and journal your successes with meditation. Read about those who gained the most from meditation.

3. Response. Make it easy. E.g., no long routines to sit and do it, meditate while standing, meditate for One Breath, do informal practice, or use the app.

4. Reward. Make it satisfying. E.g., use the Authentic Attitudes (AA), definitely rest (RA), or start with *informal* techniques to reduce stress.

What about those <u>bad</u> habits that frustrate your new meditation habit?

1. Cue. Make the cues for your <u>bad</u> habit invisible. E.g., unplug and put away the phone and TV (I put a picture in front of my TV and I forget it's there).

2. Craving. Make the bad habit unattractive. E.g., remind yourself of all the downsides, use sticky notes and diary entries, create a consequence for indulging.

3. Response. Make it difficult to get into your bad habit. E.g., restrict your access to the wine cupboard (or what helps you with your bad habit), or make it inconvenient to get involved with the internet.

4. Reward. Make it unsatisfying. E.g., instead of basking in the good feelings from your indulgence, make it clear how unhappy you are about your bad habit.

Don't Rely on Your Willpower

Make your habit of meditation as easy as possible to drop into. That means having no restrictions on where and when you can meditate. It may mean meditating with your eyes half-open, as the Tibetans do, so you can meditate while standing.

James mentions having enough cues. I have told students they should schedule the One Breath for twelve times a day. That's doable, since each meditation is only for one or two breaths. However, a *wish* to meditate (even for just one breath) isn't good enough. You need to decide on the triggers (cues).

I mentioned *breaks from the computer* as a cue to meditate. You need to decide on what activity is the trigger for your meditation. The more often, the better. Once you get that habit built, you can look at making one of those cues into a trigger for a five-to-ten-minute meditation. Later, turn it into a ten-to-twenty-minute meditation.

Motivation and willpower are fickle, so you do not want to rely on them. You can pump up your motivation by reading about meditation, or gathering with others to meditate. I've mentioned how meditation can be like a game of snakes and ladders. When you're up, you'll have the willpower to continue. When you appear to fall back, you need others, or accessible material, to uplift you. Have plans to reignite your *craving,* so you *respond* with another meditation and gain the *rewards.*

Purification

We all go through rough patches in our life and meditation practice. In the spiritual traditions, they call this purification. As you may recall, meditation releases *bubbles of stress* that rise to the surface. As we release the stress, we may feel physical, emotional, or mental discomfort. This release is how meditation is a purification process.

Not taking the *purification process* into account can ruin our new meditation habit. Recognise and celebrate every reward you receive from meditation. Appreciate every moment of peace. Write it down in your journal or diary. When the purification process gets rough, look back at how you've progressed and reignite your motivation.

Stickiness of Being Stuck

I've taken this section from the book, *Gentle Art of Intentional Awareness,* by Q.C. Ellis.

Some people – introverts especially – are good at staying focused for longer. As an introvert, I can tell you it helps us to stay focused on our studies and pay attention to the person we are with. It makes us good listeners. Introverts are also sensitive to their environment – which means we are acutely aware of how things affect us.

When you point your awareness with focused attention, your awareness will stick to it. Observing, focused on one thing, is Engrossed Attention (EA). Like being engrossed in a book or movie, EA pulls you in, cocooning you from other distractions.

When introverts (and extroverts) focus on pleasant things, the cocoon effect can take hold quickly. It then takes effort to pull oneself away. It has stickiness.

This same phenomenon can pull you in when you focus on unpleasant situations.

When you are aware of the sensations in your body associated with stress or anxiety, it is easy to continue observing. Meanwhile, your mind worries about what's wrong.

It doesn't take long before the pull of EA makes it easy to stay with those feelings. Your awareness is now sticking to the problem and the mind dutifully follows. This process makes you feel more stuck.

My advice to introverts but also for everyone: please measure how long you focus on your problems. Make sure you spend <u>more</u> time focusing on your dreams, nature, the things you love and appreciate. That's a habit I'd encourage everyone to develop.

After writing this chapter, I realise how important it is to have others we can turn to for support. That support is available through the traditions. Alternatively, I will make it possible for you to join me (and others) on the app. Join with other IntrAnaut Space Cadets who are on a similar journey. Check out how via the next chapter, *Resources And What Next?*

21

Resources and What Next?

YOU HAVE BEEN PICKING up nuggets (and hopefully some gems) throughout the book. Now it's time to cash them in and make genuine progress with your meditation. Soon, I'll tell you about the amazing things on the app. First, let's set out a path for a steady upgrade in your meditation.

What might a steady upgrade look like?

Five-Point Plan For Upgrading Your Practice

1. Decide what your most important goals are for your practice. What are they? Which meditation is best to achieve them?

2. Make it a regular practice. What present habits will you glue your habit of meditation to?

3. Overcome the obstacles. What myths will you drop, and what gems can replace them? What bad habits will you replace with meditation?

4. Make it easy. What have you decided will be your response when you encounter purification? What support will you put in place?

5. Stack the odds, and the joy! How will you enjoy life and meditation?

What Is the Best Meditation? (1)

The best meditation is the one that takes you a step closer to achieving your goals.

Spoiler alert: not every meditation will take you to the specific effects attributed to 'meditation'. The seven mind-technologies can, but only if you are using specific meditations within each sphere. This list might be helpful.

- RA + IA will reduce your accumulated stress. An antidote to trying too hard. Quieting the mind.

- RA + IA will give your intuitive mind access to the data it needs to make changes in the background. You respond to new stress more appropriately.

- RA + EA supports the release of trauma and major stress from your system. Developing focus of attention (antidote to a hyper mind).

- RA + EA sets in motion the Principle of Gravity (see below). The other mind-technologies then become a lot more effective.

- RA + AA will make all your meditations more therapeutic and your life happier.

- RA + VI is used for healing, better performance (sport or work, etc.), or goal visioning (manifesting).

- RA + QI is great for spiritual enquiry, changing beliefs, and asking what your essence wants.

- RA + MI is wonderful for opening to new ways of trusting and loving. It's also for those who are musical.

The list – of goals the seven spheres will support – is not extensive. They are initial pointers.

Glue Your Habit of Meditation (2)

In the previous chapter, we found a few nuggets about how to develop better habits.

I suggest making something you already do regularly a cue to meditate. Sticking your new habit to the end of an old habit (such as cleaning your teeth) makes it easy. Go through the chapter on habits and create a bulletproof plan to create a meditation habit.

Drop the Problems (3)

Bad habits suck your time and energy. You want to let them go. Tweak your circumstance, so there are more restrictions on picking up the bad habits.

There is no room within the spheres or principles of meditation for self-criticism. Gently get back into your capsule (RA) and restore your balance with meditation. Personally, I found it helpful to see the frustrations as purification. In this way, you reduce the impact of getting frustrated (which promotes stress).

Most stress-releasing processes (informal practices) will not release the deeper levels of stress, but at least you do not have to use your meditation time to process daily stress. Instead, you are using your meditation to open you to deeper shifts of transformation.

Use the Authentic Attitudes (AA) during every meditation (and as an informal practice) to drastically reduce the frustrations and promote better habits of mind.

Nurture Your Practice (4)

Make it easy.

The easiest way, is to make all the spheres into *informal* practices. I encourage you to do this. Hopefully, you also realise the error in thinking *informal* practice = meditation. Even if your practice is 100% *informal* for a while, that's OK. It gets you started, and I know you will want to include formal meditations soon.

Once you are past the most troublesome part (2 and 3 above) there is still a tightrope to navigate. Getting the balance right: between too much effort and too much relaxation.

During a long Tibetan Buddhist retreat, I was told of a technique I've heard nowhere else. I am calling it "Intent – Let Go". It gives you training in noticing the subtleties of too much effort versus too relaxed. You use it with the breathing meditation.

Intent – Let Go

1. On the in-breath, intend to be aware of the sensations. Have a strong intention. Notice how hard it is to not push, pull, or control.

2. On the out-breath, relax as much as you can while not completely losing contact with the breath.

How much can you let go, yet still have a glimpse of contact with your meditation?

You will quickly notice how hard it is to intend without controlling. You may find it hard to relax without letting go of the breath. That's OK. The first few minutes are almost always full of distraction. Keep doing it until the stickiness of Engrossed Attention (EA) kicks in.

Celebrate Your New Life (5)

Meditation is not about *peak experiences*. It is not about *managing your state*. It is not a *mindset*. Meditation goes beyond those things.

Author Michael Brown, of *The Presence Process*, says life isn't all about choices. Instead of an *or* attitude, we can have an *and* attitude.

You do not have to choose one form of meditation and stick to it. You can choose one or two spheres as your main practice because that will help you achieve your goals. *And* you can use all the others in various combinations to support you.

This is my recommendation – use *all* the mind-technologies, in formal meditation and informal practice. Get excited about, and play with, how you can combine them.

You read about how I stack the joy during a retreat. Play with ways you can add more appreciation, more inner smile, and more stress release to uncover the calm beneath.

Celebrate the moment you <u>notice</u> you're distracted. Celebrate the rough meditations — you've just released (purified) a heap of stress! Enthuse, "Yes!" when you have a pleasant meditation, or notice something (any sensation related to the breath) during a One Breath meditation.

These moments of appreciation and enthusiasm tell your brain that this is something *you want more of*. You're not joyful about the distraction or perceived frustrating meditation, but the *awareness* (of distractions), and *stress-release* — *which takes you one step closer to peace, wisdom, and joy.*

How Can the App Support You?

1. Decide what your most important goals are for your practice. You have a private journal built into the app, with prompts and space for you to write your decisions and experience. Use it to remind yourself of your goals and your successes.

2. Make it a regular practice. Join the FREE membership within the app and join the regular meditation sessions. Sign-up for the monthly **All One Planet newsletter** to hear about events (

https://qcellis.com/7-ways-newsletter).

3. Overcome the obstacles. Wellness experts offer advice, and resources to help. Find advice in the articles, audio, and videos. There is also a Q&A section.

4. Make it easy. There are audio recordings of meditations by several teachers. Join courses (live and recorded), challenges, and other events.

5. Stack the odds, and the joy! Get the course, *Gamma Meditation: Bliss-Out Like A Buddhist Monk*! Sign up for a retreat (virtual or in person). Use the quote gallery to inspire you.

Resources For Book Owners

The seven meditations from this book are on audio, so you can relax and let me guide you. Only book owners have access to six of the seven meditations. You will also find:

- *The Visualisation Enhancement Kit*. Get this to help you with the visual side of VI.

- *Stacking Joy*. An article and stacking joy meditation on audio. Plus, there is a course, *Gamma Meditation: Bliss-Out Like a Buddhist Monk**. Methods used by monks and nuns of the Tibetan Buddhist traditions for millennia – that induce blissful states.

- Kindness meditation. To develop a kind heart toward yourself. How much happiness will you allow yourself to feel?

- *Melt Stress In Minutes**. A short course and resource with a powerful impact on people's stress levels. I used it with people from an anxiety group who said their stress level was over 10 (out of ten). Within minutes, their distress subsided dramatically.

- How to sit cross-legged: article and video.

There is a cost to these items with a * (unless someone wants to pay for the app, and my bills?). There will be other paid-for courses, etc., available.

Plus, you'll have access to all the *free* articles, videos, meditation audios, podcasts, journals, meditation teachers, wellness experts, virtual events, and courses that are available for FREE to members. There are three memberships:

- Beginners – everyone starts here.
- Advanced – for those beyond beginner. Register when you are ready.
- Meditation Teachers (for both aspiring and inspiring MT, by application only).

Yes, there are upgrades to paid memberships available. As hinted at above, I'd love to give it all for free.

Access the FREE App Now

Point your smartphone at the QR code below (at the end of this chapter) to download the app, *Meditation & Wellbeing*.

Seven Principles of Meditation

You may have the correct impression that meditation is vast in its dimensions: it is.

Psychologists talk about the thinking mind, the subconscious mind, and the super-conscious mind. For me, this shows depth of mind. When meditating, we let go of the thinking mind to uncover the deeper levels. These are the levels where intuition, inspiration, healing, and insight come from.

The deeper levels also align with (and make easier) awakening/enlightenment (if you're interested in that). Accessing the depths of your mind can massively reduce your stress (mental, emotional, and physical), and open you to wisdom beyond the normal capabilities of the thinking mind.

One way of progressing with your meditation is to incorporate as many of the *Principles of Meditation* into your practice as possible – making none of them into a law you must obey.

There have been hints about the seven secret codes throughout the book. Not in any coherent way or to their full extent. Here, we make them explicit so you know how those tips fit into the bigger picture of meditation. The secret codes are *principles* you can use to take your meditation to mastery.

Here are the seven principles we are aspiring toward:

1. The Principle of Intention (not to be mistaken for your willpower).

2. The Principle of Mind (expansion, space).

3. The Principle of Trust, (let go, allow, surrender, and healing).

4. The Principle of Rest (calm, peace, silence, and stillness).

5. The Principle of Bliss (pleasant feelings, and enthusiasm – love).

6. The Principle of Gravity (attract toward, sticky, and absorption).

7. The Principle of Continuum (depth, breadth, and altitude – including the stages of development).

The secret codes reveal your essence. Who and what you are at your core. They are not just for intrAnauts. You do not need them before you can meditate. But the principles will help you progress in your meditation.

Each principle holds secret codes that unlock your ability to journey inward and reap the rewards of your persistence. They are the foundations that underpin every meditation, therefore, can have a profound effect on your practice.

The Overview Effect

Astronauts tell us the effect of seeing Earth in her wholeness is profound. The effect on them has several names, including the Overview Effect. Some compare the Overview Effect to a spiritual experience, as told by the wise people of ancient times.

Astronauts and cosmonauts have experienced:

> The Overview Effect is a shift in worldview reported by astronauts. ... It refers to the experience of seeing first-hand the reality that the Earth is in space, a tiny, fragile ball of life, "hanging in the void," shielded and nourished by a paper-thin atmosphere. The experience often transforms astronauts' perspective on the planet and humanity's place in the universe. Some common aspects of it are a feeling of awe, a profound understanding of the interconnection of all life, and a renewed sense of responsibility for taking care of the environment. ~ Frank White, author of The Overview Effect: Space Exploration and Human Evolution

It is not just seeing the planet from beyond the thin blue veil. Weightlessness and silence loom as the effects of gravity and sound are removed. Awe and joy are part of the mix.

They can sustain a sense of inner peace when they get back; due to recognising their troubles are minute compared to the vastness of space.

Those who are religious tend to say it is a spiritual event. Others wrestle with the change of worldview to a more holistic, humanitarian, and global awareness. Frank goes as far as to say:

> There certainly have been breakthrough experiences akin to "enlightenment" on space missions.

There are now projects planned to take community leaders into space to experience the Overview Effect.

Is the experience of astronauts related to meditation?

For most astronauts, seeing the totality of Earth from outer space has re-wired their brains. The astronauts for whom the Overview Effect had the greatest impact may have been those who had already opened their minds to new ways of thinking.

They tell us the Overview Effect goes beyond any intellectual knowledge or philosophical musings. It is a direct experience of truth that affects them at a deep, intuitive level.

For us the possibility of having that same experience – in outer space – is minimal.

Astronauts have tried to find out what happened to them. They find similar changes written about by meditators since the beginning of time. Those meditators (intrAnauts) were exploring their mind.

Instead of a space rocket, the intrAnaut has a space capsule called meditation. Instead of outer space, an intrAnaut explores their inner space. Yet, despite the difference between inner and outer, the re-wiring of the brain can be at least equal.

Do Meditators Experience The Overview Effect?

The Overview Effect is specific to those who have seen our home planet from the outside. Meditators have experienced similar effects on their worldview.

Like astronauts, there may be years of training before the big event. Like astronauts, the amount of opening you've undergone will have a bearing on the depth of enlightenment you experience.

Undoubtedly, meditation opens people to new ways of experiencing life. The cool thing is, this *side-effect* happens without having to change anything in your life – just meditate.

You don't have to become a philosopher, take religious studies, or try (pretend) to be loving and kind – just meditate.

The seven forms of meditation covered in this book will take you there. The more of these seven forms you use in your regular practice, the quicker and easier it is for results to appear.

IntrAnaut™ Academy

Did you know there are Citizens' Astronauts? An organisation takes leaders to outer space. You feel the weightlessness and see Earth from space. You see how Earth doesn't have any boundaries between the regions and experience the Overview Effect.

Well, you can have a similar thing happen on a retreat. Except we call them insights. You may gain insights that create a fundamental change in your perspective. This is the intrAnaut's equivalent to the Overview Effect.

You see your meditation and your life as a dance between relationships. The relationship between you and your body. Between you and your mind. You notice the dance between the infinite space of your mind and the outer world.

Longer retreats are the quickest and easiest way of creating your luxury space capsule and becoming a true intrAnaut.

You now have your space boots, and become an IntrAnaut Space Cadet. Well done! I look forward to seeing you on the app and in person on a retreat.

TO DOWNLOAD THE APP, point your phone at the QR code below. You can also access the download page via the internet at:
www.**MeditationWellbeing.app**

With your **Android** Smartphone, point your camera at the QR code and choose your QR code reader (e.g., Google Lens), to be taken to Google Play.

With your **Apple** Smartphone, point your camera at the QR code and choose your QR code reader, to be taken to Apple Store.

How do you get your exclusive resources?

1. Open the app, go to the Menu [≡] and tap 'Unlock Code'.

2. Type this code into the Tracking Number box: **866718**

3. Press TRACK NOW button and you will see a page asking for your name and email address. Type those in and touch the Submit button.

You are now a FREE member, but also have access to the book owner's resources.

After registering, you will receive the monthly All One Planet newsletter and some emails from me to welcome you and help you get the most from the app.

The newsletter gives you hints and tips about meditation. Plus, updates on new articles, books, and events to support you in your practice. If you cannot access the app, subscribe to the **All One Planet newsletter** to access the material and courses via websites. www.**qcellis.com/7-ways-newsletter**

Glossary

Meditation

Meditation is a purposeful activity of mind, with seven principles and making use of the two core, or more, of the seven technologies.

MEDITATION IS LIMITED TO an activity of the mind. You're not meditating if your activity includes anything other than the mind or less than the first two spheres of meditation (see also, *Formal Practice* and *Informal Practice* below). The seven spheres/forms/mind-technologies are:

Restful Absorption (RA)

Intentional Awareness (IA)

Engrossed Attention (EA)

Authentic Attitudes (AA)

Visualisation or Imagination (VI)

Question or Introspect (QI)

Mantra or Invocation (MI)

Seven Spheres, Mind-technologies, or Forms of Meditation

These terms relate to the seven mind-technologies of all meditations, as defined in PART TWO, and briefly described below. Together, the seven make up the new framework for understanding meditation.

Restful Absorption (RA)

A core mind-technology within every meditation. Ideally, you are at rest, which means you are still and completely relaxed. You are relaxing enough for absorption to take effect.

Absorption – is what happens when you fall asleep, and can be mapped to the four brainwave frequencies (states) as described by science: *Beta* (normal awake state), *Alpha*, *Theta*, and *Delta* (fully asleep).

When your mind becomes calm, through RA, you can more effectively connect with your imagination, creativity, inner wisdom, and intuition. Absorption is the main ingredient in meditation that releases accumulated stress.

Cocoon Effect – is your meditation capsule – when absorption creates a comfortable space, in which you are undistracted. When RA is combined with EA, you can meditate for longer when cocooned in absorption.

Intentional Awareness (IA)

A core mind-technology within every meditation. Moment-by-moment conscious awareness. You are being aware on purpose. It can be called *bare awareness, with nothing added*, so you are not intentionally thinking about what you are aware of.

Thoughts are allowed to be there, but ideally, you are not engaged in thinking. Sounds can be heard, but ideally, you are not actively listening.

IA is a training that emphasises being present with whatever you are aware of. Because it is a training, we do not make the ideals into rules.

Engrossed Attention (EA)

EA steadies your IA (see above) in a narrow-focused attention. It uses introspection and memory to steady your focus on one object. EA has you know the details through a finer and finer degree of focus, creating more conscious awareness.

Engrossed – relates to the special relationship this technology has with absorption. It gets harder to draw yourself away from the object of your focus. It also helps you to relax deeply without falling asleep. The recommended object to train in EA is the breath.

Authentic Attitudes (AA)

Completely natural attitudes everyone possesses. They include curiosity, being gentle toward yourself, allowing, kindness, and others. Strengthen an attitude with an AA meditation, or use them within all your meditations.

Neutral Zone – you are without positive or negative opinions.

Gentle – an energetic/supportive inner-environment where rest, or time-out, is available for you. Relax away from the negative thinking for a moment, and relax in a tender, forgiving, understanding, and soft manner.

Beginner's Mind – is being *curious* about what may appear in your awareness. You're *open* to the possibility of your assumptions being wrong, which means putting them to one side, while you treat your experience as an experiment. It takes *courage* to let go of the old and welcome the new.

Allowing – (aka acceptance) the present moment and everything in it, to be as it is. The present moment has already come into existence. Once you have noticed it, it is already in the past. Accept it already exists, and you cannot change the past.

Appreciation – you look for something within your environment (external or internal) to appreciate. By that, I mean you can say "That's OK." It is a recognition and enjoyment of the good qualities of something, but that thing can be tiny. You are allowing yourself to experience beauty — no matter how small.

Kindness – to be kind toward yourself, to a certain extent, is simply to not judge yourself. Kindness arises spontaneously at this stage on the AA — from being gentle, curious, allowing, and appreciating.

See also, *Distorted Attitudes*, below.

Visualisation or Imagination (VI)

You are using your imagination. VI is especially broad in its uses. For instance, you can use VI for healing purposes or better performance (e.g., in sport). VI doesn't have to be visual images in your mind.

Question or Introspect (QI)

You are contemplating, asking questions, or introspecting. Although this sounds like an analytical thought process, that part of the meditation is minimal. The emphasis is on the opening to intuition. We find this form of meditation within some types of prayer or insight/wisdom meditations.

Mantra or Invocation (MI)

Within the context of meditation, a mantra is a tone, or set of syllables, that have shown positive effects. A MI is used to invoke specific frequencies within your mind. The *informal* practice of MI is *chanting*. Depending upon your goals and preferences, there are many MI available.

Object of Meditation

The primary focus of your awareness. The object is what you are directing your attention toward, and attempting to notice something about it.

Formal Practice

Sitting, lying down, or standing still and completely focused (as best you can) on your meditation practice.

Informal Practice

When you are doing other things, you can partially use the mind-technologies. Informal practices to either:

1. Prepare you for meditation (e.g., walking, while engaging RA, IA, and AA).

2. Help you gain extra time in training.

Both are so the results of your *formal* practice will be greater. Using the mind-technologies to improve your *other* activities is also *informal* practice. Unfortunately, many people conflate *informal* practice with *formal* meditation.

Distraction

The object of meditation is no longer within your awareness. You have forgotten your intention and are now involved with something else. It could be distracting thoughts, emotions, or physical sensations.

Your distraction could be something pleasant, desirable, or uncomfortable. Either way, you are completely distracted away from your meditation. See *Bubbles of Stress* for the biggest reason for being distracted.

Bubbles of Stress

The reason why people have distracted minds is due to stress being released.

The analogy used, is that a bubble of accumulated stress rises to the surface during meditation. When it hits the surface, the bubble bursts and releases the stress. The release (bursting of the bubble) disturbs your (energy, physical, emotional, mental) systems and this creates a *distraction*.

Wandering

You are <u>not</u> *completely* distracted. Your object is in the background and you're still aware of it. Maybe you're more interested in something else, or a part of your mind seems to be. Your mind has wandered, but not completely away from the object of your meditation.

Slumber

You become *less* conscious instead of *more* conscious during meditation. The cocoon effect of absorption is taking effect but you are drowsy – heading toward (unconscious) sleep.

Attitude

Our reaction – towards a thing, person, and oneself – is what we usually call an attitude. Defined as *a learnt tendency to evaluate and react to things in a certain way*.

Distorted Attitudes

A lifetime of accumulated stress causes the imbalance that creates distortions in your thinking, attitudes, and emotions. There are five main distorted (weather) patterns of attitude.

Whistling Wind of Cynicism – a scoffing, incredulous, cynical, sceptical mind. Pessimistic, pedantic, suspicious, distrusting, and jaundiced by life.

Foggy – a blank screen of confusion, leaving you feeling disoriented with an empty mind.

Weeping Cloud, feeling Emotional/Sensitive/Distressed/Anxious – feeling sad, upset, anxious or depressed, crying for no reason, and even the positive emotions feel too intense.

Stormy/Thunderstorm – maybe a minor storm of frustration, annoyance, irritability, impatience, or exasperation. Clouds of displeasure, dissatisfaction, simmering resentment, bitterness, or agitation may follow you. Or full-blown anger, outrage, wrath, or a temper tantrum may strike.

Whirlwind/Typhoon/Cyclone/Tornado – a hyperactive mind, with a never-ending stream of thoughts, continually projecting into the future with strategising, evaluating, assessing, creating, narrating, rehearsing, imagining, or worrying, etc. Or ruminating on the past, by remembering, re-hashing dramas, establishing meaning, blaming, etc. You feel as if you cannot calm your mind.

IntrAnaut

A person who wants to explore the inner space of their mind so as to awaken to their true potential. There are various stages of training and mastery as an intrAnaut. IntrAnaut™ is a TradeMark owned by Colin Ellis and used by IntrAnaut Academy and Meditation Teacher College with permission.

About the Author

Meditation Maverick

Q.C. Ellis is the pen name of Colin Ellis. Colin is known for teaching practical methods to awaken his clients' natural restorative abilities and fire up their inbuilt happiness – using meditation as the primary tool.

People know Colin as a:

- Author and meditation teacher.

- Coach, mentor, and facilitator.

- Founder of Meditation Teacher College.

- Lead Trainer at IntrAnaut Academy – on the mobile app and retreats.

Colin says he basically does two things:

1. Facilitates personal evolution (incl. awakening) via 1-on-1 coaching or on meditation retreats.

2. Most of the awakening journey is healing and letting go of the beliefs and stress (in all its forms) that keep us down/asleep. Therefore, he facilitates releasing and untangling through coaching, leading-edge psychotherapies, intuitive healing, and meditation.

His 1-on-1 service is called *Beyond Willpower*. To grow beyond your limitations, you need to go beyond mindset and the use of willpower.

The *IntrAnaut Academy* supports people to engage with meditation in a fun way.

The *Meditation Teacher College* is for aspiring and inspiring guides, who wish to join Colin in his mission to *awaken as many people as possible during the evolution in consciousness* happening on the planet right now.

Colin has been studying personal and spiritual development for as long as he can remember. Initially, he was looking for ways to help himself overcome a lack of self-esteem, anxiety, and become more confident. In his teens, he became interested in human potential once he had trained as a Royal Marine Commando.

Later, his goals were in pursuit of peace, contentment, and joy.

Colin has explored meditation and mindfulness for decades, with many teachers – including Venerable Mahayana and Theravada monks while on retreat. In fact, he has been on longer retreats than some monks.

Students say his approach is *understated, yet he engenders trust* because of his deep insights and hard-won knowledge. He comes across as a quiet, inspiring, cheeky monk rather than a motivational speaker.

He would be the first to admit he made too many mistakes in his practice to count. At least it means he can guide others to avoid them. He knows from experience why certain approaches are unhelpful (not just because he read it's a bad idea).

He feels driven toward being a part of the human evolutionary shift (awakening), so has explored many avenues of personal and spiritual development – as a retreat participant, student, coach, therapist, and teacher.

Colin says:

> *Thank you for investing in yourself, and I hope you gained at least **one valuable insight** from reading this book. I'm eager to improve so I'd love to hear from you about what you found frustrating in this book. I also love seeing people develop, so please let me know if you found this useful. Use the connection links below and get in touch!*

Author website: www.**QCEllis.com**
Connect with Colin via social media and find out about his latest adventure via: www.**ColinEllis.info**

Get updates via the All One Planet newsletter:
www.**QCEllis.com/7-ways-newsletter**

Please Review This Book on Amazon

Of the 100s of meditation books, people want to know if this one is worth the read... What's your honest opinion?

If you found this book useful, please take a couple of minutes to write a short, honest review on Amazon. It just needs to be a sentence or two.

You can see reviews by others (from on and off Amazon), on the book's website at www.**7WaysToMeditate.com**

Acknowledgments

With Immense Gratitude

Individuals

All My Students, *without whom I would not have learnt half as much as I have about the nuances of meditation*

Gordon, Sally, David, and Corina. *My parents and siblings*

Barry & Emma McGuinness *Enlightenment Intensives, Bath, UK*

Lama B. Alan Wallace, PhD, *author, and founder of the Santa Barbara Institute for Consciousness Studies and the Center for Contemplative Research*

Venerable Tharchin, *a highly regarded monk in the NKT (Tibetan Buddhism)*

Bhante Bodhidhamma, *Satipanya Buddhist Retreat (vipassana, insight meditation, in the Mahasi Tradition)*

Norma Foster, *International Growth Consultant, and Therapeutic Coach*

Mike Saville, *University of Fools (the Fool's Journey)*

Rikki Blyth, *Author, Astrologer, and Artist*

Carlos Caldeira, *CEO of NET 360 CIC, and Tennis Coach to young athletes turning Pro*

Helen Whitehead, *Shamanic (Dance) Facilitator and Movement Medicine (apprentice)*

Emma Berry, *Artist and Maker (e.g., museum quality artefacts)*

Lisa Hatton, *Transformational Breath®, Thai Massage, Clinical Hypnotherapist*

Shakti Tracy, *Diamond Heart Network (Shamanic Journeys & Breathwork)*

Susan Lancaster, *Therapeutic Bodywork Massage and Meditation Teacher*

John Quinn, *Creative Wellbeing Practitioner*

Terry & Jill Gregg, *of The Garden Station, Northumberland, UK*

Lyn Wareham, *who is an awesome Beta Reader*

Organisations

Land of Joy, *a retreat centre in Northumberland, UK, where I did my latest three-month solitary retreat*

The Newcastle Dance Collective, *providing me with Movement Medicine, 5 Rhythms, and other opportunities to let my body talk and heal*

ActionEra, *who developed a mobile app platform for experts (and created my app)*

Joint Venture Insider Circle (JVIC), *providing me with a platform to collaborate with other experts*

Anxious Minds, *the charity where I was their Mindfulness Teacher*

Printed in Great Britain
by Amazon